THERE
IS
MORE!

THE SECRET TO EXPERIENCING GOD'S
POWER TO CHANGE YOUR LIFE

RANDY CLARK

© 2013 by Randy Clark

Published by Chosen Books
11400 Hampshire Avenue South
Bloomington, Minnesota 55438
www.chosenbooks.com

Chosen Books is a division of
Baker Publishing Group, Grand Rapids, Michigan

Printed in the United States of America

Library of Congress Cataloging-in-Publication Data

Clark, Randy, 1952–
    There is more! : the secret to experiencing God's power to change your life / Randy Clark ; foreword by Bill Johnson.
        p.   cm.
    Includes bibliographical references and index.
    Summary: "Bestselling author helps believers truly understand how God's grace and presence empowers them to do more, change lives, and live in a supernatural way"—Provided by publisher.
    ISBN 978-0-8007-9550-4 (pbk. : alk. paper)
    1. Anointing of the Holy Spirit. 2. Change (Psychology)—Religious aspects— Christianity. 3. Supernatural (Theology) 4. Powers (Christian theology) I. Title.
BT123.C53 2013
234´.13—dc23   2012034823

The internet addresses, email addresses, and phone numbers in this book are accurate at the time of publication. They are provided as a resource. Baker Publishing Group does not endorse them or vouch for their content or permanence.

Cover design by Gearbox

13   14   15   16   17   18   19   7   6   5   4   3   2   1

In keeping with biblical principles of creation stewardship, Baker Publishing Group advocates the responsible use of our natural resources. As a member of the Green Press Initiative, our company uses recycled paper when possible. The text paper of this book is composed in part of post-consumer waste.

I dedicate this book to the people who laid hands upon me and from whom I received an impartation. In chronological order, they are John Wimber, Blaine Cook, Rodney Howard-Browne, Benny Hinn, Omar Cabrera Sr. and Carlos Annacondia.

In addition, I dedicate this book to the many people whom I have laid hands upon, who have received a sovereign impartation from God and have gone forth empowered by His grace and tangibly demonstrating His love to people.

And finally, I dedicate this book to my wife, DeAnne, and to my children: Josh and his wife, Tonya, Johannah and her husband, David Leach, Josiah and his wife, Allie, and Jeremiah. And, of course, to my grandchildren, Simeon and Selah.

Contents

Contents

Foreword

Few people in modern history have had the kind of effect on the Church around the world that Randy Clark has had. His humble approach to ministry and his abandonment to the move of God have kept him on the cutting edge of revival.

There are times when God gives an impartation to an individual. I have received that when Randy has laid hands on me. And yet, there are times when an impartation is given to a whole church. Such was the case during Randy's visit to Redding. The impartation he brought to Bethel Church impacted hundreds of us, and we have never been the same since.

One of the greatest privileges of my life has been my friendship and partnership with Randy. The impartation that he received has been passed on to countless others, who are now changing their world. As I tell our young people, at least four other giants were killed in the Bible besides Goliath—and they were all killed by men who followed David. If you want to kill giants, follow a giant killer.

And that is the story of impartation.

Pastor Bill Johnson, Bethel Church,
Redding, California

Introduction

There is more! This "more" is the reality of God drawing near, rending the heavens and coming down. It is the difference between times of revival and times of decline in the Church. Revivals are led by people who have been touched by the "more," whether that experience is described in the language of entire consecration, sanctification or baptism in the Holy Spirit. Periods of revival are characterized by people who believe the life they are living and the things the Church is experiencing are beneath what is possible and available in God. This belief causes them to seek Him for an impartation of more.

This book is about the impartation of that "more." But what exactly is the more? It is many things: more love for God and humankind, more power, more anointing, more joy, more burden of the Lord for the lost, more revelation from God regarding the needs of others, more conviction over sin, more faith in prayer, more conversions, more gifts, more healings, more deliverances, more churches planted and more of the culture being leavened by the Kingdom of God.

People who have received impartations of God's enabling graces become history makers. They may not always become national or international history makers, but they change their personal history and the history of those around them at the local church and community level. A powerful impartation produces fruit for the Kingdom of God. It is not a matter of talk, but a demonstration of power.

The impartation experience I am speaking about is not just receiving a blessing from God. Neither is it a matter of being strengthened by the Holy Spirit or by an angel. It is more than that. There is destiny connected with the impartation. Many times it is accompanied by a prophetic word that reveals this destiny. At other times, a person's destiny has already been revealed to them, and later they receive an impartation that enables them to accomplish that God-given destiny.

The following pages are full of testimonies that attest to the title of this book, *There is More!* In writing this book, I hope to stir up a greater hunger for this "more" of God. Many Christians, especially in the Western Church, do not even know that there is more beyond the routines of their church culture. As you read these pages, I hope that you will desire to experience more of God's empowering presence, desire to receive a personal impartation and desire to be more powerfully used by God in your local church, your community, your city and the world.

PART 1

The Reality of Impartation

For this reason I remind you to fan into flame the gift of God, which is in you through the laying on of my hands.

~ 2 Timothy 1:6

Again Jesus said, "Peace be with you! As the Father has sent me, I am sending you." And with that he breathed on them and said, "Receive the Holy Spirit."

~ John 20:21–22

1

The Biblical Foundation
for Impartation

Is there a biblical precedent for the impartation of anointing? Is this doctrine and practice a part of our orthodox Christian heritage, or is it just a bizarre blip on the time line?

These questions about impartation stir up a whole range of opinions and cause controversy that still swirls around today's renewal movement. It is my heart's desire to provide some common ground in the area of a scriptural and historical understanding of impartation, with the aim being to "make every effort to keep the unity of the Spirit through the bond of peace" (Ephesians 4:3).

The writer of Hebrews clearly considers "the laying on of hands" as so basic to the Christian life that he refers to it as foundational and as an elementary teaching of the apostolic Church:

Therefore let us leave the elementary teachings about Christ and go on to maturity, not laying again the foundation of repentance from acts that lead to death, and of faith in God, instruction about baptisms, *the laying on of hands*, the resurrection of the dead, and eternal judgment. And God permitting, we will do so.

Hebrews 6:1–3, emphasis added

The Bible teaches in both the Old and New Testaments the principle of a person receiving an anointing from God. This anointing may be a gift or gifts of the Spirit, a filling of the Holy Spirit (especially for power) or the baptism in the Holy Spirit. This idea of impartation or transference of anointing is a strong biblical concept. In Brazil, where I frequently minister, the best translation of the English word *impartation* is, in fact, the phrase "transference of the anointing." I believe this understanding will be helpful for those who are unfamiliar with the term *impartation*.

As we look at biblical examples, we see that this anointing often came through the laying on of hands. But let me make an important clarification: The laying on of hands is certainly not the *only* way of receiving an impartation from God. It is simply one of two ways seen in Scripture. The other way is waiting on God through prayer. That second way is a means often forgotten and neglected by the Church, so I have therefore emphasized it a number of times in this book.

Old Testament Impartation

Let's take a look at some Old Testament passages documenting this idea of impartation. The first reference to the concept of impartation is in Numbers 11:16–18 (emphasis added):

> The LORD said to Moses: "Bring me seventy of Israel's elders who are known to you as leaders and officials among the people. Have them come to the Tent of Meeting, that they may stand there with you. I will come down and speak with you there, *and I will take of the Spirit that is on you and put the Spirit on them*. They will help you carry the burden of the people so that you will not have to carry it alone."

This passage makes no mention of Moses laying his hands on the elders for them to receive, but the concept of a transference of the anointing that is on one man to the others is clearly present. Equally evident from the Numbers text is the principle that this is not something man can do; it is an act of God, totally dependent on *His* calling and anointing.

In Deuteronomy 34:9, again we see a transference of anointing: "Now Joshua son of Nun was filled with the spirit of wisdom because Moses had laid his hands on him." This time, specific mention is made of Joshua receiving or being filled with the spirit of wisdom *because* Moses laid hands on him. With or without the actual laying on of hands, though, the transference of anointing is clearly a biblically documented, God-initiated event.

Another example is found in 2 Kings 2:9–15, the famous passage that tells of Elijah's anointing being transferred to his spiritual son, Elisha. This passage indicates that it is possible to receive an anointing similar to that of another person. When Elisha begged, "Let me inherit a double portion of your spirit" (verse 9), he was not asking for the power of Elijah's human spirit, but for the Spirit of God to work through him as it did through his teacher. Likewise, when the people said, "The spirit of Elijah is resting on Elisha" (verse 15), they did not mean that Elisha had received power literally from the spirit of the man Elijah, but that the Spirit of God was indeed working through Elisha in a powerful way similar to what they had witnessed in Elijah.

New Testament Impartation

New Testament examples also reflect the two ways we can receive power, gifts, anointing, fillings or baptisms in the Holy Spirit. As I said, one of the ways is through praying and waiting on God, and the other is through the laying on of hands. What did the "laying on of hands" refer to in Hebrews 6:1–3, which I quoted at the start? Several things: the act of ordination, healing and/or blessing and, significantly for us, impartation. Let's look at each of these, along with some Scripture connected to them.

The Act of Ordination

First Timothy 4:14 is most likely a reference to Timothy's ordination. "Do not neglect your gift, which was given you through a prophetic message when the body of elders laid their hands on you." And 1 Timothy 5:22 is most likely another reference to the laying on of hands and ordination. "Do not be hasty in the laying on of hands, and do not share in the sins of others." The same thing is found in Acts 6:6, in what many consider to be the ordination of the first deacons. "They presented these men to the apostles, who prayed and laid their hands on them."

The first commissioning or ordaining service for missionaries is recorded in Acts 13:1–3, especially in verse 3. "So after they had fasted and prayed, they placed their hands on them and sent them off." As we later see with Timothy, these services were not mere rituals, but were the occasions when the Holy Spirit imparted gifts and empowered believers for ministry. Also, these gifts were often accompanied by prophecies.

Healing and/or Blessing

The laying on of hands was not just for ordination, but also for healing and/or blessing. Matthew 19:13–15 (emphasis added) tells us,

> Then little children were brought to Jesus for him *to place his hands on them* and pray for them. But the disciples rebuked those who brought them.
>
> Jesus said, "Let the little children come to me, and do not hinder them, for the kingdom of heaven belongs to such as these." When he had *placed his hands on them*, he went on from there.

This particular reference does not say whether Jesus placed His hands on the children for blessing or for healing, but we know that Jesus did both. Mark 10:16 is a passage that clearly refers to Him laying His hands on people for blessing. "And he took the children in his arms, put his hands on them and blessed them." Another passage, Mark 5:23, this time clearly refers to Jesus laying His hands on someone for healing. Jairus pleaded earnestly with Jesus, "My little daughter is dying. Please come and put your hands on her so that she will be healed and live," and Jesus did so.

Although Jesus healed in many ways other than the laying on of hands, many gospel references connect the laying on of hands to the ministry of healing. Here are some examples:

He [Jesus] could not do any miracles there, except lay his hands on a few sick people and heal them.

Mark 6:5

He took the blind man by the hand and led him outside the village. When he had spit on the man's eyes *and put his hands on him*, Jesus asked, "Do you see anything?"

He looked up and said, "I see people; they look like trees walking around."

Once more *Jesus put his hands on the man's eyes.* Then his eyes were opened, his sight was restored, and he saw everything clearly.

Mark 8:23–25, emphasis added

When the sun was setting, the people brought to Jesus all who had various kinds of sickness, and laying his hands on each one, he healed them.

Luke 4:40

Then he put his hands on her, and immediately she straightened up and praised God.

Indignant because Jesus had healed on the Sabbath, the synagogue ruler said to the people, "There are six days for work. So come and be healed on those days, not on the Sabbath."

Luke 13:13–14

The disciples were also to follow the example of Jesus and lay their hands upon the sick for healing. Mark 16:18 says of believers, "They will place their hands on sick people, and they will get well." In Acts 28:8–9, Paul followed the practice of laying on of hands for healing. On the island of Malta, a man was sick in bed, suffering from fever and dysentery. "Paul went in to see him and, after prayer, placed his hands on him and healed him. When this had happened, the rest of the sick on the island came and were cured."

Paul not only ministered healing, but he also received healing through the laying on of hands:

> Then Ananias went to the house and entered it. *Placing his hands on Saul*, he said, "Brother Saul, the Lord—Jesus, who appeared to you on the road as you were coming here—has sent me so that you may see again and be filled with the Holy Spirit." Immediately, something like scales fell from Saul's eyes, and he could see again. He got up and was baptized, and after taking some food, he regained his strength.
>
> Acts 9:17–19, emphasis added

Although it is not expressly stated, this passage seems to imply that Paul not only received healing, but also the infilling of the Holy Spirit when Ananias laid hands on him.

Impartation

Another aspect of the doctrine of laying on of hands is connected to impartation. The impartations we see in the Bible were both for gifts of the Spirit and for being filled with or baptized in the Holy Spirit. Luke is the historian of the Holy Spirit. I believe he wrote his gospel of Luke and the book of Acts with consideration for the theological significance of the history he was recording. In Acts he recounts more than one instance where people were filled with the Holy Spirit *without* any mention of the laying on of hands:

> When the day of Pentecost came, they were all together in one place. Suddenly a sound like the blowing of a violent wind came from heaven and filled the whole house where they were sitting. They saw what seemed to be tongues of

fire that separated and came to rest on each of them. All of them were filled with the Holy Spirit and began to speak in other tongues as the Spirit enabled them.

Acts 2:1–4

"Now, Lord, consider their threats and enable your servants to speak your word with great boldness. Stretch out your hand to heal and perform miraculous signs and wonders through the name of your holy servant Jesus."

After they prayed, the place where they were meeting was shaken. And they were all filled with the Holy Spirit and spoke the word of God boldly.

Acts 4:29–31

While Peter was still speaking these words, the Holy Spirit came on all who heard the message. The circumcised believers who had come with Peter were astonished that the gift of the Holy Spirit had been poured out even on the Gentiles. For they heard them speaking in tongues and praising God.

Then Peter said, "Can anyone keep these people from being baptized with water? They have received the Holy Spirit just as we have."

Acts 10:44–47

In Acts 2 and 4, the Holy Spirit came on believers who were looking to God for enabling power. In Acts 10, as Peter preached for the first time to the Gentiles, the Holy Spirit came on everyone who heard the message, even as they were being saved.

Note also that the Day of Pentecost was not the day when the disciples *first* received the Holy Spirit, but rather the day when they were *filled* with the Holy Spirit. According to John 20:21–22, the disciples *first* received the Holy Spirit when

Jesus breathed on them on the evening of His resurrection day. "Again Jesus said, 'Peace be with you! As the Father has sent me, I am sending you.' And with that he breathed on them and said, 'Receive the Holy Spirit.'"

More pertinent to our topic, however, are Luke's accounts of where the Holy Spirit or gifts of the Spirit were imparted *with* the laying on of hands. In Acts 8:14–17 (emphasis added), we read about the revival in Samaria:

> When the apostles in Jerusalem heard that Samaria had accepted the word of God, they sent Peter and John to them. When they arrived, they prayed for them that they might receive the Holy Spirit, because the Holy Spirit had not yet come upon any of them; they had simply been baptized into the name of the Lord Jesus. Then Peter and John *placed their hands on them*, and they received the Holy Spirit.

Apparently, the giving of the Holy Spirit was accompanied by some visible manifestation, because Luke continues with the reaction of Simon the sorcerer in verses 18–19. "When Simon saw that the Spirit was given at the laying on of the apostles' hands, he offered them money and said, 'Give me also this ability so that everyone on whom I lay my hands may receive the Holy Spirit.'"

The second such passage involving impartation with the laying on of hands is found in Luke's theological-historical account in Acts 19:6. Paul, rather than Peter and John, places his hands on newly baptized believers in Ephesus. "When Paul *placed his hands on them*, the Holy Spirit came on them, and they spoke in tongues and prophesied. There were about twelve men in all" (emphasis added).

In both of these stories, Samaria and Ephesus, it is significant that the experience of receiving the Holy Spirit came *after* the experience of believing. Some teach that the baptism in the Holy Spirit happens at salvation, but one is hard-pressed to prove this from the writings of Luke. It did not happen that way in any of his passages we have discussed so far. These are all references from the earliest history of the New Testament Church that deal with when and how people received the Holy Spirit or that indicate what it looked like when the Spirit "came upon" or "filled" believers. The focus of these events is a distinct *impartation* of the Holy Spirit, rather than the regeneration of the Holy Spirit that occurs at salvation.

In Romans 1:11–12 we again find the concept of impartation. This time it is for the impartation of some spiritual gift to the Christians at Rome. Paul writes, "I long to see you so that I may impart to you some spiritual gift to make you strong—that is, that you and I may be mutually encouraged by each other's faith."

The activity of the Holy Spirit was vital to Paul's understanding of his role as an apostle. At the end of his letter to the Romans, Paul emphasizes the connection between his proclamation of the word and the empowerment of the Spirit. He states in Romans 15:17–19,

> Therefore I glory in Christ Jesus in my service to God. I will not venture to speak of anything except what Christ has accomplished through me in leading the Gentiles to obey God by what I have said and done—by the power of signs and miracles, through the power of the Spirit. So from Jerusalem all the way around to Illyricum, I have fully proclaimed the gospel of Christ.

In this passage, Paul seems to understand that the effectiveness of his ministry was not simply the result of what he preached, but of what he did as well—"by the power of signs and miracles, through the power of the Spirit."

I am indebted to Dr. Gordon Fee, who brought to my attention that the apostle Paul's most foundational doctrine was the experience of the Spirit as the basis for the certainty of one's salvation. The basis for an assurance of one's salvation is the realization of God's empowering presence in one's life. The experience of God's empowering presence was even more foundational for Paul than justification by grace through faith. Being justified by grace through faith was Paul's second most important foundation of belief. Dr. Fee writes,

> Indeed, the experience of the promised eschatological Spirit, not righteousness by faith, forms the core of Paul's argumentation in the one letter (Galatians) devoted primarily to this issue. The death of Christ brought an end to the curse of the law—that one had to live by "doing the law" and thus not "by faith" (Gal. 3:10–14). The gift of the Spirit makes the law's function of identifying God's people obsolete. "Those who are led by the Spirit," Paul says, "are not under 'Torah'" (5:18). For those in whom the fruit of the Spirit is growing "there is no law" (v. 23). For Paul the Spirit thus marks the effective end of Torah. How so? Because the Spirit is sufficient to do what Torah was not able to do in terms of righteousness, namely to "fulfill in us who walk by the Spirit the righteous commandment of Torah" (Romans 8:4).[1]

With such an emphasis on receiving the empowering presence of God through His Spirit, and the realization that the presence and activity of the Holy Spirit was the true source of his own fruitfulness as a minister of the Gospel, it should not surprise us to see Paul wanting to come to the Romans to impart to them some spiritual gift. Nor should it surprise us to see Paul reminding Timothy, his beloved son in the ministry, to "fan into flame the gift of God, which is in you through the laying on of my hands" (2 Timothy 1:6).

For Paul, Timothy, Peter, John and by logical inference, the entire early Christian Church, the impartation of anointing through the laying on of hands was an important catalyst for effective ministry characterized by the manifest presence of God, and for operating in the complete gifts of the Holy Spirit. It was this first Church—small, despised and poor— that changed the world!

God has promised another final and radical outpouring among the nations before His Son returns. Again, He will bring it about through His people. Jesus said, "As the Father has sent me, I am sending you" (John 20:21). If we are to walk in this high calling, we can neither forget nor neglect the resources of heaven made available to those who are humble and hungry enough to receive. God is not looking for the well financed, the well educated nor even the well experienced in "ministry." He is simply looking for those who are willing to yield their hearts and lives to all He wants to do working through them. He is looking for those who are willing to believe for more, because there is more!

Having considered the reality of impartation from the biblical perspective, now let's consider it from the personal perspective. In the next chapter, I want to share with you how God brought me personally into such an understanding of impartation. I will share my journey of how God powerfully touched me and changed my life. There is much more to my story than I share here, but because the focus of this book is impartation, I will concentrate on the parts of my story that involve my growth in that area. It is important to know that I was not raised in a charismatic or Pentecostal church or denomination. It is the grace of God that has made it possible for me to understand impartation. I did not enter into these things because of my will, but by God's grace. But before I move into my story, let me pray for you.

Lord, create right now in the person who is reading these pages a hunger for the "more"—more of an impartation of Your Spirit and Your gifts. Create faith in this reader to receive gifts through impartation, and to receive a new and stronger filling of Your Spirit through impartation. I ask this in the authority and power of the name of Jesus, Amen.

2

A Man Made Ready

My Testimony of Impartation

In January 1984, two deacons from my church and I attended the James Robison Bible Conference in Dallas, Texas. Up until that time, I had only had one dream in my life that I absolutely attributed to God, so the dream I had the night before the conference really caught my attention. I have never forgotten it. Through the dream, I knew God was telling me (and my congregation) that He wanted to take us into a closer relationship with Him and into a higher realm of His Spirit. With each phase would come a higher accountability and more things in my life that I would have to surrender to Him—things He would reveal to me at each time of transition.

The second day of the conference we attended, John Wimber taught a session for about five hundred pastors. I was amazed at all the words of knowledge he gave, and I loved what he was saying. I was watching on the front row as he had many people come up on the stage. As a Baptist, I knew how to recognize when someone was under conviction, but I had never before seen the power of God move visibly and physically on people. As John prayed for one woman, he said, "Watch her. See what the Spirit's doing."

My deacons and I watched and saw the hem of her dress begin to shake. I said, "Do you see that? Her dress is shaking!" I know now that it sounds funny to be excited about something as small as a lady's hem shaking, but this was all new to me. The woman began to shake even more, then she touched someone else, and they began to shake. People were getting healed, and the whole thing was a wonderful experience.

That same day, God used David Yonggi Cho's message at the conference to convict me of my need for more intimacy with God and a relationship with the Holy Spirit. All afternoon, I did not want to be around anyone as the Lord dealt with my heart. I went back to the meeting that night, though, and David Wilkerson spoke. The pastors came forward and were on their faces repenting, crying out to God. TV cameras from Trinity Broadcasting Network were rolling, however, so I did not want to kneel or put my face on the ground. Everybody was weeping and crying, but I was thinking, *Man, this is being beamed back to Marion, Illinois, and they'll see it.*

I knew that thinking was just pride on my part, so I finally knelt down and prayed a little bit. When I stood up and began singing a song, I felt as though the Spirit of the Lord said, "Raise your hands up!"

Now, I was a Baptist, and we did not do that! But I raised my hands up, and as soon as I did, the Spirit of God hit me.

I immediately knew I was in trouble, and I felt ready to lose it emotionally. I looked around and then headed for a big projection screen because I thought I could hide behind it. As soon as I got to it, the Spirit hit me again. I fell against the wall, tried to grab hold of it, slid down and ended up lying on the floor. The bottom of the screen was about three feet off the floor, so there I was, visible to everyone. I lay there shaking and crying for about half an hour. Then I got up and started back to my chair. Before I could even take two steps the Spirit hit me again, and I slid back down the wall into a heap on the floor and wept and cried and shook some more.

One of my deacons told me later that they were asking each other, "Where's Randy?" Finally, one of them pointed up front to where I was lying underneath the screen in front of about eight thousand people.

The next night I went up to John Wimber. I did not feel worthy of asking for prayer for myself, so I asked him to pray for my deacons. As I turned to get them, he caught my hands, looked right into my eyes and said, "No, I want to pray for you."

Knowing he had been having words of knowledge, I felt so exposed. I expected the worst to come out of his mouth. It was the first time we had ever met and he did not know anything about me, yet he said, "I want to pray for you, but first I want to pray for your heart because you've been wounded lately in your church."

It was the truth. A couple of months earlier I had been terribly hurt by the church, so I knew this was from the Lord. John then spoke several things to me, including, "You're a prince in the Kingdom of God."

I did not know what to do with that. I felt like anything but a prince in the Kingdom of God.

Then he said, "There's an apostolic call on your life."

I did not learn until ten years later that when John used the term *apostolic call*, he meant that I would end up one day having a ministry that involved traveling. John did not believe, however, that because you traveled you were apostolic, and neither do I. This seems to lose the meaning of *apostolic*. It means that God has sent you, that you have been called to wherever He sends you and that you will often be used in activating gifts or imparting gifts wherever you are sent. And neither John nor I believe that only apostolic ministry can be used for impartation. Ananias in Acts 9 was not an apostle, just a member of the church, yet God sent him to lay hands on Paul.

John also shared many other good prophecies with me, and I went away encouraged. I also went away with a new impartation in my life for words of knowledge, as well as a greater hunger for God than I had known in years.

A couple of months later, in March 1984, we held a healing conference at our church. John Wimber's Vineyard team arrived with speaker Blaine Cook. Both my wife, DeAnne, and I struggled with pride and unbelief when it came to the manifestations we witnessed going on around us during this conference. It actually scared us a bit to watch people receive impartations. We were not used to seeing the power of God touch people in such ways. I did not really know what was going on, and I understood very little about the spiritual gifts. Still, I had given my authority to Blaine and told him to go for anything that he thought was of God.

During the first evening session, Blaine prayed for both DeAnne and me. The power of God came on both of us, and together we received an impartation from God that gave us boldness. What happened during this experience of impartation? It was so powerful that I no longer considered what happened in Dallas as an impartation. I felt like I had grabbed hold of an electric wire. I began to shake, feeling electricity flowing through my body. It was so strong that the next day all my joints ached. The anointing of God had a similar effect upon my body, as the electricity was so strong I could not control the shaking. It also activated the gifts of words of knowledge and healing in our lives in much greater measure. Others in our church received impartations for various gifts as well, and we witnessed many healings.

One of those who was powerfully touched, a layman, was John Gordon. His experience was so powerful that, to this day, I tell about it almost every time I teach on impartation. (May something similar happen to you as you are reading *There Is More*.) You will read more about John in chapter 8.

I would have one more powerful impartation in the 1980s. After 43 years of ministry, I have had only these three most precious, most life-changing experiences. I pray often for another. The second one was in 1989. I had left the Baptist church and joined the Vineyard movement in September 1984 to start the first Vineyard church in St. Louis. Five years elapsed, and I was confused about what I was here for, what my main calling was. John Wimber had told me there was an apostolic call on my life. The prophet Bob Jones had told me I had a teaching gift. I was a pastor. My first love was evangelism. I told the Lord to have someone come to me and prophesy to me, clarifying what my main calling was so I could focus on it. God answered my prayer.

What happened on that occasion? I was told that one day I would travel the nations, that my son would travel with me—but he would not ride my coattails. Rather, I would ride his because his anointing would eclipse mine. This prophecy stunned me, as I had never left the United States. I sat, saying nothing in response to the regional overseer who had given me the prophetic word. A few minutes later I thanked him for sharing such a powerful word with me. I then asked him to pray for me. When he did, another regional overseer from the Vineyard blew on me. I fell to the floor, instantly feeling tremendous heat, which caused me to sweat profusely. My hands became electrified, and I felt electricity around my mouth. I was crying loudly, at first screaming from the sensation of power. Lying at first in a fetal position, I felt as though someone grabbed my hands and someone else my feet and began to stretch my body. I couldn't feel my hands any longer, and it felt like my face was being electrified, especially around my mouth. I remember fearing I would die if this energy increased. There was so much power in my hands that they hurt. This lasted about 45 minutes, but for another hour I couldn't let my hands down past my waist because they hurt so badly if I did.

The anointing one receives in an impartation has to be stewarded, or the power can begin to diminish. Even good stewardship doesn't guarantee the season of revival will last forever, because it isn't just an individual issue; there is a corporate responsibility in the culture of a local church.

Walking in New Places

So much happened over the next eighteen months after our initial impartation at the Spillertown Baptist Church in southern Illinois. God taught us how to walk in a whole new realm of the Spirit. The rain of the Holy Spirit that we experienced at the Spillertown Baptist conference was like a flood in those first months. The second experience of impartation was also profound, with life-changing consequences, especially in regard to freedom from a besetting sin. Then the flood went to an occasional shower, and by the time nine years had passed since the initial outpouring in the Baptist church, I found myself and my Vineyard church in the midst of a desert time. I desperately cried out to God, and He answered my prayers. In His wisdom, He sent me to a Rodney Howard-Browne conference at Rhema Bible Church in Tulsa, Oklahoma. I was not in agreement with some of the ideas coming out of this particular church, but I sensed that my attending was a test from God at the time, so I went.

During the first few days of that conference, I was uncomfortable with the Holy Spirit manifestations that I saw going on around me. I knew, however, that I did not want to return to St. Louis until God had touched me. On the last day, when the call came to go forward to receive, I could not get to Rodney because of the 4,500 other people crowding to the front. In desperation I cried out again to God, asking Him to touch me even if it meant my shaking, rattling and rolling around. I went to a hallway to get in line and wait for Rodney to lay hands on me. When he did, suddenly I found myself on the floor, unable to get up!

This happened five times when Rodney laid hands on me, and it was during these times that God changed my heart. I repented of my mean spirit and realized how displeased God is when we take the attitude of attacking Christian brothers over issues that would not be considered heresy. I also received a powerful impartation that changed my life.[1]

When I returned to my church in St. Louis, things exploded. Every Sunday following my return, we had a powerful outpouring of the Holy Spirit—this in a church that had never experienced anything like it in its eight-year history. The power of the Spirit fell, bringing powerful manifestations and deep changes in people. I also attended our regional meeting of Vineyard pastors, and I asked the Lord to touch the pastors there who were as desperate as I was. The second night of the meeting, God moved sovereignly and everyone got blasted! People were running around dancing, slapping each other on the back, rolling around and generally acting drunk. Happy Leman, my regional overseer, was laughing hysterically. When I saw Happy, typically a nondemonstrative "Mr. Control" type, doing that, I knew it was God!

Then my area pastoral coordinator, who was already drunk in the Spirit, asked me to pray for him. I agreed even though he had already been prayed for twice. I touched him, and it was as though the Spirit of God hit him and knocked him into some chairs. He said it felt as if a truck had hit him. I did not know he had a severe spinal injury that caused him to wake up in tears every morning from the pain. I also did not know that he had been told there was no hope for correcting it surgically. When God came on him, he said it felt as if a hot hand went down in his stomach and pulled something out, and he was healed! The anointing of God was on him, and he could not talk for months without stuttering. He stuttered all the time when the Spirit of God would come on him. God had done a wonderful thing for him.

The Toronto Blessing

A pastor in Toronto, John Arnott, heard about these meetings and invited me to come speak at his church in Toronto, the Airport Vineyard Christian Fellowship. I agreed to come for four nights, but I was nervous about the expectations he and his church might have. Deep down, I still struggled with having faith that God would do for me what He did for others. Before I left for Toronto, however, God gave me a powerful word of prophecy—even though I did not place a high value on prophecy at that time. I received a phone call from Richard Holcomb, whom God had had praying for me for over a decade. Richard would also send me funds from time to time without my ever mentioning any financial need, and each time the amount was exactly right! Since Toronto, Richard has been on my board for Global Awakening, but at the time he knew absolutely nothing about what had been happening in my life or about my planned trip to Toronto. This is what he said to me:

> The Lord says to you, Randy, "Test Me now. Test Me now. Test Me now. Do not be afraid. I will back you up! I want your eyes to be opened to see into the heavenlies My resources for you, just as Elisha prayed for Gehazi's eyes to be opened. And do not become anxious, because when you become anxious, you can't hear Me."

It was this prophetic word that did so much to change my life. It gave me the faith to move in the anointing I had received when John Wimber prayed for me ten years earlier and when Rodney prayed for me. I went to Toronto, and what happened for 42 of the next 60 days there is now a part of Church history called the Toronto Blessing.

I just want to say that ushering in this revival was not something Randy Clark did; God did it all. In His desire to take failure and turn it into His strength, God orchestrated events that touched my life and drew me into new places. I had pastored in St. Louis for eight years, and my church was only averaging about three hundred people. Some saw this as a failure, and so did I. I was not a successful pastor; I was a broken man. I also had a black mark against me because of a divorce back when I was 22. In spite of all this, God chose to use a simple man like me. God chose a manger, humble surroundings and a poor mother and stepfather for His only Son, too.

God gave me the faith to respond to His divine invitations, of course, and to cooperate with them. I believe that nothing powerful happens without God's initiative in grace, but I also believe that His invitations are conditional upon human response to that divine initiative. I do not want to minimize the importance of our human response—if I had not been willing to respond in God-given faith to what God was doing, He would have found another vessel to use instead of me. Both divine, sovereign grace and initiative *and* human response and cooperation are necessary and important.

That is the story of how God prepared me for the work that was to break out into something far bigger than I ever expected. If you want to know more about how God prepared me for ministry and about my involvement with the Toronto Blessing, you can read my book *Lighting Fires* (Global Awakening, 2011). Suffice to say here that God put new values in me, empowered me and healed me of doubt and fear. He also brought me before men who would help me. I am so grateful to the men of God who believed that their anointing was something to be given away through impartation. It is my sincere conviction that all God has entrusted to me is to be given away to others, until the whole Church is built up, equipped and empowered by the fullness of the Spirit, to the glory of God.

3

How to Receive an Impartation

I have given much thought to the conditions that might be prerequisite to receiving an impartation of the Holy Spirit—if there are any conditions. It seems to me that possibly, the first condition is to become aware of our personal inadequacy in our Christian life. We must recognize that our lives are characterized by too much defeat, along with our indifference, a lack of power, a lack of faith . . . We must come to the place of facing our weaknesses and our inability to affect the work of the Kingdom.

We may be well trained to do "church work," run committees, preach or teach, administrate and counsel, all through our education. But that is not the same as the ability to heal the sick, cast out demons, raise the dead and preach with an anointing that breaks down hard hearts with such conviction that people are brought to Jesus. These things need the anointing, the grace and the gifts of the Holy Spirit. So the first condition prerequisite to impartation is to recognize our need, our spiritual poverty. Jesus said, "Blessed are the poor in spirit, for theirs is the kingdom of heaven" (Matthew 5:3).

Second, I think we must desire for our spiritual condition to change. By this I mean that we must allow the Holy Spirit to develop a serious desire in us to become victorious Christians. Some people cannot even conceive of the possibility of living victoriously rather than living in defeat. This is because they, and even some commentators, view Romans 7:14–26 as an indication that Paul's experience as a Christian was defeatist:

> We know that the law is spiritual; but I am unspiritual, sold as a slave to sin. I do not understand what I do. For what I want to do I do not do, but what I hate I do. . . .
>
> So I find this law at work: When I want to do good, evil is right there with me. For in my inner being I delight in God's law; but I see another law at work in the members of my body, waging war against the law of my mind and making me a prisoner of the law of sin at work within my members. What a wretched man I am! Who will rescue me from this body of death?
>
> Romans 7:14–15, 21–24

This usually Calvinistic viewpoint is counterproductive to the hope of living victoriously. I highly recommend that you not accept it. Instead, I recommend that you read Dr. Gordon Fee's chapter in my book *Power, Holiness and Evangelism* (Destiny Image, 1999), which takes the opposite view—that Paul taught us we could live a life of victory by the power of the Spirit rather than a defeated life. Dr. Fee powerfully states that a defeatist view of Romans 7 completely contradicts everything else Paul wrote about life in the Spirit. The same Holy Spirit who can develop the desire in us for a victorious lifestyle can also provide the faith for such an experience and the faith to continue in that lifestyle. Allow the Holy Spirit to let you see the truth of Scripture on this matter.

A third prerequisite to receiving impartation is a desire within us that our lives honor God and that we be used in His service, for His glory. We do not ask for a spiritual high to make us feel good or for an experience that can boost our ego or spiritual pride. Rather, we ask for the power and gifts to make us commensurate to the task before us—that of binding our enemy the devil and plundering the kingdom of darkness. As Matthew 12:29 says, we need to be empowered and prepared: "Or again, how can anyone enter a strong man's house and carry off his possessions unless he first ties up the strong man? Then he can rob his house."

The task before us is that of breaking down the gates of hell. Jesus told Peter, "And I say also unto thee, That thou art Peter, and upon this rock I will build my church; and the gates of hell shall not prevail against it" (Matthew 16:18, KJV). In our victory God is glorified, honored and pleased. This empowering by the Holy Spirit enables our faith to express itself in love. Dr. Billy Graham wrote,

> I think it is a waste of time for us Christians to look for power we do not intend to use; for might in prayer, unless we pray; for strength to testify, without witnessing; for power unto holiness, without attempting to live a holy life; for grace to suffer, unless we take up the cross; for power in service, unless we serve. Someone has said, "God gives dying grace only to the dying."[1]

Unity in Diversity

I am excited about what I see happening right now in the Church. Since I traveled to Toronto and began those meetings years ago, meetings that continued six nights a week for twelve and a half years, I have been privileged by God's grace to meet key leaders of both the evangelical and Pentecostal streams. I am finding that there is much more openness to a diversity of spiritual experiences now than there was twenty years ago. I am finding Pentecostals open to working with me even though they know I do not believe one must speak in tongues to be baptized in the Spirit. (I have had a prayer language since 1971, but it did not occasion my baptism in the Holy Spirit.) At the same time, I am finding evangelicals who are open to working with me even though they know I do believe that the gifts of the Spirit and baptism in the Spirit can occur simultaneously with conversion, though in reality they are almost always subsequent to it. I am finding men of evangelical stripe who admit that they were baptized in the Holy Spirit *after* their conversion, and I am meeting Pentecostals who admit that they believe a person can be baptized in the Holy Spirit either *before, after or at the same time as* one receives one's prayer language.

In summary, the traditional walls are beginning to fall. Long-standing "prerequisites" for spiritual experiences such as impartation are no longer seen as such hard-and-fast rules. Why? Because desperation has arisen in the hearts of many to experience what the Bible speaks of in such experiential terms, rather than being satisfied with a less hands-on, but tidier, supposedly theologically correct understanding of the baptism in the Spirit or other types of impartations.

While I was in training at the Southern Baptist Theological Seminary in Louisville, Kentucky, one of my professors was Dr. Lewis Drummond. He told about the great Shantung Revival that took place among the North China Mission of the Southern Baptist Convention in 1932. I graduated in 1977, but I did not read about the Shantung Revival for another nineteen years, not until I began to have an impression in my mind that I needed to get my hands on anything written about that revival and read it. When I finally read *The Shantung Revival* by Mary Crawford,[2] I was captivated. Her report made it clear that the revival began among leadership who were tired and burned-out. They admitted their need for *more*, and they discovered that some leaders among them were not even truly born again. In fact, some referred to Shantung as the "born-again revival" because a deeper understanding came through it about what true conversion really is, so that some of the missionaries discovered they had not yet been born again.

The emphasis of the revival was a study of the Bible relating to the Holy Spirit and the baptism in the Holy Spirit, along with studying the meaning of true conversion. Phenomena like shaking, falling, crying and laughing occurred in the Shantung Revival. Many healings also occurred. Many people who received an impartation of the Holy Spirit took this fresh anointing and were used in other parts of the province. These same things seem to occur everywhere that people seek the fullness of the Holy Spirit. I have found evidence of this in Protestant revivals all over the world, from Roman Catholic histories of revival and in the Bible.

Two Approaches to Impartation

As I have studied the history of the Church, there appear to be two approaches to appropriating impartations. The first is to try to pursue holiness as a matter of conquering sin. In this approach, when one becomes "sanctified," one then becomes eligible for a powerful impartation. This can be traced back to the asceticism of the desert fathers, the monks who deprived their fleshly desires even to the point of denying basic needs. This conquering the flesh or subjecting the flesh to the Spirit is seen in the writings of the "Holiness" groups from John Wesley until today, but especially in the 1700s and 1800s, right up into the early 1900s. This is the model for the "three-stage" Pentecostals who came into Pentecost out of the Holiness denominations such as the Church of God-Cleveland, the Pentecostal Holiness and others. The three-stage Pentecostals believed that the first stage was conversion, the second stage was sanctification as a "second *definite* work of grace"[3] that was instantaneous and the third stage was the baptism in the Holy Spirit. These three-stagers were the ones who left the Methodist denomination to form new Holiness denominations over the issue of this "second definite work of grace" distinct from salvation, which gave a person victory over inbred sin.

The two-stage Pentecostals, on the other hand, believed the first stage was conversion, sanctification was a process and the second stage was the baptism in the Holy Spirit. These were the more reformed or Baptistic types of Pentecostals. They believed sanctification was already ours in the finished work of Jesus.[4] Actually, about 25 new denominations were founded during the first 14 years of the Pentecostal movement.

About half of the membership were three-stage, the other half were two-stage, and about one-fourth of all Pentecostals were "Jesus only" and did not accept the doctrine of the Trinity.[5]

Why is the difference between a three-stage and a two-stage Pentecostal important to our discussion of impartation? It is because impartation is a major theme of the Pentecostal message, and the most important impartation is that of the filling with or baptism in the Holy Spirit. It is also because the stages people believe in affect their expectation levels. Theological and biblical perspectives have a controlling factor in people's faith. If you do not expect to receive certain gifts until after an experience of sanctification, you usually will not receive them. But if you believe it is possible to experience the gifts after conversion or at conversion, then there is faith present to receive the gift or the impartation.

What one expects to receive filters the experience. If one expects victory over previous sinful habits (sanctification), then faith is present for this experience. If people have faith to receive power and begin to move in a particular gift without first having a holiness experience, they will experience the Spirit in relationship to what they were already experiencing. Within the Church, there are millions today who hold either the two-stage or three-stage view of the filling with or baptism in the Holy Spirit—an impartation. There are millions who come from the Holiness or Pentecostal camps for whom this is a real issue—enough so that these camps parted ways over it in their formative years, choosing an either/or option rather than a both/and. "Second definite work of grace" was a Holiness Wesleyan phrase that meant sanctification, but the phrase "baptism in the Holy Spirit" was preferred over sanctification or "second word of grace" in the last twenty years of Wesley's life. So when the Pentecostals said the evidence of the "baptism in the Holy Spirit" was tongues for the purpose of boldness to witness, this was like invalidating the Holiness view that the baptism in the Holy Spirit was for moral transformation and gaining victory over indwelling sin. The earliest Pentecostals were Holiness and saw the baptism as another experience available to those who already had the "sanctification" second work of grace; this was the third work of grace. When these camps did not value each other's views, it closed each out to the truth or important emphasis the other had. Our choice is not an either/or, but a both/and.

The second approach to receiving impartations is by faith in the "finished work" of Jesus—meaning He has already made me holy, and He is my sanctification. What I need to do is reckon this as truth in my life. Then I receive my sanctification, baptism in the Spirit and impartation of gifts by faith. Striving is removed, and resting in faith takes its place. This is the more Calvinistic approach within the Holiness movement. Though received by faith, however, the evidence is experiential—the experience is the assurance that genuine faith has prevailed.

Phoebe Palmer exemplified this view. She pioneered a form of "confess what the Word says is yours, and then claim this experience by faith in the word of God." She was a Methodist, and thousands came into the experience of sanctification through her teachings, which came to be called the "shorter way."[6] The Keswick movement[7] also represented this view of sanctification as a finished work, but still emphasized the need to confess any unforgiven sin prior to receiving the baptism in the Holy Spirit.

This second approach, receiving by faith in order to appropriate an impartation, is the one that has allowed more people to enter into or receive their experience of impartation. Note that there is some truth, however, in the first approach we talked about, that of pursuing holiness by conquering sin. Some of the men and women who crucified their flesh and sought God for both purity and power did become very anointed for healing. But in my opinion, it was not because of their asceticism that they moved in this power, but because of their hunger for God and His power, and because of their intimacy with God.

Regardless of our theological tradition, whether it is more Methodist/Holiness or Reformed/Baptistic, we all need to have the experience—we all need to be filled with or baptized in the Holy Spirit. I am more concerned that we have the experience than I am that we have the best, most theologically correct way of talking about the experience.

Evangelical Insight into This "Issue"

At the end of this chapter, I want to give you some practical guidelines for receiving an impartation that I hope will help you a great deal. I will talk about some specific things you can do (or not do) while being prayed for that will make it easier for you to receive from God. Before I do that, though, in the hope of helping as many people as possible be able to receive, I want to look at this "issue" of being filled with or baptized in the Holy Spirit from one more perspective. It is not an issue for those within the Pentecostal or Holiness traditions, but it poses more of a problem for those in the evangelical position (especially the cessationist evangelicals), so I want to draw some insights here from two famous evangelicals, Dr. Billy Graham and Dr. Harold Lindsell.

I trust you know who Dr. Graham is, but not everyone may know Dr. Harold Lindsell's reputation. Dr. Lindsell was editor emeritus of *Christianity Today* at the time he wrote the book from which I will be quoting, *The Holy Spirit in the Latter Days*. He received his Ph.D. in history from New York University and his D.D. from Fuller Theological Seminary. For more than twenty years, he served on the faculties of Bible colleges and seminaries. He was a prolific author and editor. Let's look at some insights from both these men in regard to the baptism in the Holy Spirit.

Dr. Billy Graham's Insights

Dr. Billy Graham places an extremely high value on being filled with the Spirit. In his book *The Holy Spirit*, Dr. Graham devotes a whole chapter to the subject "How to Be Filled with the Holy Spirit." He wrote,

> I am convinced that to be filled with the Spirit is not an option, but a necessity. It is indispensable for the abundant life and for fruitful service. The Spirit-filled life is not abnormal; it is the normal Christian life. Anything less is subnormal; it is less than what God wants and provides for His children. Therefore, to be filled with the Spirit should never be thought of as an unusual or unique experience for, or known by, only a select few. It is intended for all, needed by all, and available to all. That is why the Scripture commands all of us, "be filled with the Spirit."[8]

Dr. Graham also lists three conditions for being filled. The first is that we must understand certain truths of the Bible. One truth we must know is that God has given us His Holy

Spirit and that He indwells us. This must occur at conversion in order for conversion to be genuine. Dr. Graham says, "*We accept this fact by faith.*"[9]

Let me note here that although I agree with Dr. Graham that faith and not works is the means of appropriating the forgiveness of God in Christ, I do not agree that the focus of faith is accepting the fact of being filled with the Spirit by faith. It is at this point that Wesley and today Dr. Gordon Fee would also have a different emphasis than Dr. Graham. They would both state that the evidence of genuine faith is the reception of the Spirit as an experience. (This is Dr. Fee's emphasis in his book *God's Empowering Presence.*[10]) Wesley believed that we are saved by grace through faith and justified by faith, but that this is not the same experience as being filled with the Spirit. One can be justified with little emotion or feeling to show for the experience, but when one is sanctified/baptized in the Spirit, it is a powerful experience subsequent to justification. Wesley believed that one could feel assurance of justification only by receiving the baptism in the Holy Spirit, being filled with the Spirit, being sanctified or by the second work of grace—all different names for the same experience. However, he was adamant that justification is not dependent upon this subsequent experience.[11] Without this distinction, the evangelical world is using the same hermeneutic principle the Word of Faith movement uses in regard to healing, claiming something that has not yet manifested in their bodies. I believe it is important for healings to manifest to make certain that we have what we have believed for. In the same manner, it is best to have evidence of the manifestation of our claim of receiving the Spirit. I am not speaking of the manifestation of a particular gift, but the realization of the evidence that the Spirit Himself has come to dwell in us. The reception of the Holy Spirit at conversion should be self-authenticating—and even more so when we are filled or baptized in the Holy Spirit.

Along with understanding certain truths of the Bible, the second truth Dr. Graham says we must understand is that God commands us to be filled with the Spirit and that it is His will for us to do so. Dr. Graham says, "to refuse to be filled with the Spirit is to act contrary to the will of God. . . . Just to make it even clearer—God *wants* to fill us with His Spirit."[12]

When it comes to the third truth, we must understand that Dr. Graham was influenced by the Keswick holiness movement. This was also the position of my evangelism professor at the Southern Baptist Theological Seminary, Dr. Lewis Drummond. Dr. Graham and Dr. Drummond were both believers in the Keswickian experience or way to obtain this filling. The emphasis was non-Pentecostal, but very similar to the "shorter way" of the Methodists. (I spoke with Dr. Drummond about this personally.) This third understanding is in regard to the presence of sin in our lives. Dr. Graham stated that sin blocks the work of the Holy Spirit in us, and that we must "deal honestly and completely with every known sin" before we are filled.[13] It becomes clear from his text that Dr. Graham is not referring here to a quick sentence confession such as, "Father, I ask You to forgive me of my sins for Jesus' sake." Instead, he means to thoroughly allow the Holy Spirit to search our hearts and bring awareness to us of every sin that we are walking in so that we specifically confess it. He writes,

We must not be content with a casual examination of our lives. . . . We must confess not only what we think is sin, but what the Holy Spirit labels as sin when we really listen to His voice from the Word of God. . . . We must not only be honest about the various sins in our lives, but we must get down to the deepest sin of all—our failure to let Christ rule our lives. *The most basic question any Christian can ask is this: Who is ruling my life, self or Christ?* . . . It is amazing how many Christians never really face this issue of Christ's Lordship, and yet the New Testament is full of statements about Christ's demand for our full commitment.[14]

Dr. Harold Lindsell's Insights

We can shed further light on our subject by summarizing Dr. Harold Lindsell's position on how to be filled with the Holy Spirit and considering some of his most important observations. Dr. Lindsell believes this:

> . . . all believers are sealed, indwelt, and experience the sanctifying grace of the Spirit in them. But not every believer is, at the time of the new birth or even later, necessarily filled or controlled by the Holy Spirit. The filling of which we speak is certainly the believer's birthright. It belongs to him or her because he or she is a child of God and a joint heir with Jesus Christ. It is the Father's wish that all of His children be filled with the Spirit. It is *a blessing that must be claimed.*[15]

Dr. Lindsell lists five things that need to happen for a person to be filled with or baptized in the Holy Spirit. First is the necessity of being born again. Second is the necessity of being under the Lordship of Christ. Third is the necessity of confessing and repenting of all sins in one's life. Fourth is asking God to fill us with the Holy Spirit. Fifth is claiming the promise.[16]

Dr. Lindsell also writes that the believer's attitude toward receiving the infilling of the Spirit can be summarized by six statements: (1) The Spirit's fullness is the Christian's birthright and belongs to a person by way of promise in the covenant of redemption. (2) After Pentecost, the promise of the Spirit was available to all believers. (3) Believers are aware whether they have the Spirit's fullness. If one does not know for sure, then one does not have it. (4) It is evident from Scripture that no one can secure this fullness by his or her own efforts, nor can it be bought. (5) Whatever the price, each sincere believer should obtain the Spirit's fullness. (6) God always keeps His Word, so believers can be certain that if they meet the conditions set down for receiving the fullness of the Holy Spirit, they are sure to receive it.[17]

Dr. Lindsell's position on claiming the promise sounds similar to Phoebe Palmer's, the nineteenth-century Holiness teacher whom I already mentioned. She moved the emphasis away from the long-standing mortifying the flesh and achieving greater levels of consecration, and then receiving the "second work of grace" for sanctification. Instead, she moved the emphasis toward believing and confessing the truth until one possessed the truth. Dr. Lindsell continues,

> The believer who asks God to fill him or her with His Holy Spirit should do so with certain biblical facts in mind and heart. The first is that it is the will of God for each believer to be filled with the Spirit. If this is so, then it is something that can be prayed for without contingency, because whatever is the will of God can be asked for with the certitude of faith.[18]

Dr. Lindsell quotes 1 John 5:14–15, "This is the confidence we have in approaching God: that if we ask anything according to his will, he hears us. And if we know that he hears us—whatever we ask—we know that we have what we asked of him." He then summarizes his thoughts by saying,

> Every believer who serves Christ as Lord, who has repented of and confessed all known sin, and who has asked to be filled with the Holy Spirit can claim the promise of God in faith. . . . The Promise of God is kept even when there may be no sign at all. We are not to look for an experience. We are simply to accept the promise by faith, and begin to thank God for what He has already done.[19]

God Makes His Own Exceptions

Though I think the positions of Dr. Graham and Dr. Lindsell are noble and generally correct, I have to admit that I do not agree 100 percent with the issue of conditions. As I reflect upon these great men's positions, I am aware that I have seen things happen with the Spirit that did not fit their conditions. I have seen exceptions to the conditions, especially the condition of a person having every known sin confessed and repented of prior to receiving the infilling or baptism in the Spirit.

I think that God makes His own exceptions, and that they are signs that this is not about performance, but about grace-based gifts appropriated through faith. Even as I wrote that last sentence, I realized that sometimes impartations are totally sovereign visitations that come where there is still need of confession and repentance, and where there is little or no faith. I have seen people who have not confessed every known sin receive impartations for power and gifts that came solely by grace.

I do agree that the three things Dr. Graham mentions—that we must understand certain truths of the Bible, that God commands and wills for us to be filled with the Spirit and that we must deal with every known sin—are important to growing in our relationship with God. But sometimes God sovereignly touches someone in the church who everyone knows does not have his or her spiritual life together. The reason God does this is to remind us that we all receive by grace. His gifts are "charismata," not "worksmata." This helps us stay in the place of gratitude and praise for His grace toward us.

In other words, when we are in a meeting where someone is ministering who is used of God for impartation, nobody is safe! In fact, that is part of chapter 8's title up ahead, where I will talk about that more. God can pour out His Spirit on anyone. The norm, however, is that He touches those in public who have been crying out in private for His impartation.

Putting It into Practice

Now that we have talked about being ready to receive the Holy Spirit (and how sometimes we are not "ready," but receive anyway since God makes His own exceptions), let's look at the practical side of receiving from God. Let me conclude this chapter with some very practical instructions regarding receiving different types of impartations. I will begin and end with a note of caution. Do not take this advice and these insights and turn them into laws. They are patterns I have seen, but please do not limit God to my limited insights. However, I do hope these insights might give you a starting place to begin to understand better how to enter into the presence of God and/or receive an impartation from Him.

I refer here to several aspects of receiving. Sometimes it can involve receiving power, other times peace, other times healing. Sometimes a person will receive all of these blessings or several of them at one time. In helping people who had difficulty receiving, I learned a lot from John Arnott. He found it difficult to receive, so both John and I have sympathy for those left standing in ministry times. We both have had similar experiences. I was left standing once years ago, when Mahesh Chavda prayed for me at Kansas City Fellowship. I was one of only two left standing out of about two hundred pastors who received prayer. John was left standing at one of Rodney Howard-Browne's meetings in which hundreds of other pastors had fallen.

I do not want to limit or categorize falling, shaking, laughing or some other type of movement to mean a specific thing. It would be foolish to limit God in such a manner. However, I would be less than honest if I did not share that some things occur often enough so that we notice common patterns in how many people respond to the Holy Spirit. For example, when people are receiving blessings of peace, they often have a tendency to become weak and fall. On the other hand, those receiving blessings of power often feel power in their hands or some other part of their bodies. They also often shake as a result of this power. Sometimes they bounce up and down for long periods of time, which we call pogoing. Sometimes the power is so strong that they fall and shake on the ground. When anointing for healing comes, they often feel heat or electricity in their body. Other times they simply feel the pain disappear.

When it comes to healing, we often have to tell the people that after the first wave of power comes on them, they need to stay focused—often God comes in waves, with pauses in between to allow the person receiving prayer a breather. This is something you can really appreciate because often the intensity of the experience is so powerful and demonstrative that a rest or pause is needed. Helping someone stay focused in an atmosphere of receptivity is important. Too many people have become used to quick prayers of pronouncements that they are to believe or stand for, and few are used to waiting upon the Holy Spirit to actually effect the healing they have asked for.

As far as falling down, I often will instruct people in a meeting the following way: "We do not desire any courtesy drops tonight. That would be the flesh. However, if you try to stand, that is the flesh also. Don't try to fall; don't try to stand up. Both are flesh."

One of the problems many people have is that of analysis. Borrowing from some instructions I often heard John Arnott give in the early days of the Toronto outpouring, I would instruct people to "get out of analysis and into romance." I would also add, as John did, "Experiencing God is a thing of romance, not analysis. Analysis *ruins* it. For example, did you know that the human mouth has more germs in it than any other part of the human body? Why would two adults put their mouths together with all those germs? Because they are not in analysis; they are caught up in romance. What you need to do is quiet your spirit and pucker." (Humor often helps lift the pressure people put on themselves.)

Another area that deals with receiving is what to do after you have fallen. I have found that too many people get up too quickly. Sometimes the anointing is so strong that a person cannot move. Other times it is not that strong. However, we quench the Spirit by getting up when He is resting on us with His peace. I instruct people to continue to lie on the floor until it is not difficult to move. Stay on the floor until you do not feel heavy and until it takes no more willpower than normal to get up.

One of the most difficult things is to get people to stop praying when they are being prayed for. This is especially true for those who have been in the church a long time and for certain types who feel it is important to pray in tongues when receiving or to say something like, "I believe, I believe; I receive, I receive." I have found it much more difficult for people to receive impartations of power for ministry that may include certain gifts while they are praying and claiming.

Obviously, I do not discourage someone who desires the gift of tongues from praying or letting the Spirit move him or her to pray without utilizing "normal" language. But I prefer to see the gift of tongues come without any instruction on what to do to prime the pump, so to speak. For example, I do not encourage anyone to start saying the names of Japanese cars to get started. I take the pressure off and tell people their prayer language may come when I pray for them, or it may come as they are driving down the highway or mashing potatoes or worshiping later on. The point is that they ask, believe, rest and receive.

I hope what I have written here will help you. I caution you against turning my observations into laws rather than leaving them as observations. At best, I consider them principles. I admit that God uses other people in a way very different from what I have talked about, and it really is God. Do not make my observations and suggestions into Saul's armor for a young David, which did not fit well at all. If God has blessed you in the use of the sling, then use it. I am simply sharing how I use my sling. My counsel to people when I minister to them is to work with the sling God has given them. It could prove counterproductive to try to use my sling if God has equipped you to minister in a different manner. So do not hear me saying I have something better than you. I am just sharing what works for me.

In part 2 just ahead, we will take note not just of the numerical fruit in numbers of churches planted, numbers of churches renewed or numbers of people brought into the Kingdom, but also of the fruit in individuals who receive impartations. We will see what the impartations they received did to them, and we will look at the primary reason for impartations—they bring a resultant increase in signs and wonders, and in evangelistic fruit. We will also see that ultimately, the reason for any impartation is so that God will be glorified.

PART 2

Into the Harvest Field

Fruit That Will Last

You did not choose me, but I chose you and appointed you to go and bear fruit—fruit that will last.

~ *John 15:16*

Ask the Lord of the harvest, therefore, to send out workers into his harvest field.

~ *Luke 10:2*

4

The Fruits of Impartation

Psalm 1 gives us a beautiful picture of impartation and its fruits in a person's life. In it we see a man who has turned away from the things of the world and the flesh and instead finds his delight in the Lord. As he meditates on the Lord's instruction day and night, he becomes like a tree planted beside streams of water, that bears its fruit in season and whose leaf does not wither. Whatever he does prospers. Isn't this what happens when we receive impartation from God? I think it is. God begins by preparing our hearts, turning us away from the things of the world and creating in us a great and desperate hunger for Himself. He answers the cry of our hearts by drawing us deeper into relationship with Him, and then He touches us so profoundly that we are forever uprooted from our old lives and replanted by streams of His living water, where we bear fruit in season. He causes us to prosper and produce fruit for His Kingdom.

In the following pages, you will read stories of ordinary men and women who have found themselves engaged in extraordinary things as a result of an impartation from God. They have been radically changed, convicted, equipped and launched with the ability to take hold of God's calling on their lives. They have come to find out that impartation has a price. It can mean enduring resistance from family, friends and even church, and it can often bring on persecution and great trials. Some have had to change their doctrine after an impartation. They have gained boldness and confidence they never could have imagined. They have found themselves being used by God to heal the sick and raise the dead.

As you read these amazing stories, you will see God's involvement and know that it is Him these believers seek. It is about knowing His heart, taking time with Him and seeing His glory. As Dr. Denise Meisburg says in one story you are about to read, "You can't use His power unless you know His heart!"

Touched by God

Rolland and Heidi Baker are long-term missionaries in Mozambique, Africa. God has connected my ministry with theirs, specifically as it relates to impartation. Let me begin in 1997, where our stories meet. After fifteen years of serving in the slums of Indonesia, Hong Kong and London, and also serving eighteen months among the broken children of Mozambique, Rolland and Heidi were in desperate need of a fresh touch from God. I believe that just as God set up a divine appointment for Cornelius in Acts 10, who also served God's people, God also set up a divine appointment for Rolland and Heidi that would take place in Toronto, Canada.

Rolland had visited Toronto before Heidi, making his first trip in October 1995. He was profoundly touched by God in the revival. Returning to Mozambique, he knew he needed to take Heidi back to Toronto with him. In July 1996 she agreed to go for the Healing Conference. On the plane, Heidi cried out to God, praying, "God, if You don't touch me, I am so tired that I'd like to just take a job at Kmart. I don't think I can continue in ministry without You touching me afresh." She was very sick at the time, and her doctor had advised her not to travel. A woman named Sharon Wright prayed for Heidi at the conference, and she was completely healed.

The Bakers returned to Toronto in the fall of 1996, and God again touched Heidi. Then in January 1997, Heidi made her third trip to Toronto. I was there at the revival as one of the guest speakers. I preached a message that I have preached many times since called "Pressing In." This is the sermon I have seen God use to build faith for an impartation of fresh anointing of the Holy Spirit all over the world. Its bottom-line message is that God is looking for people who are desperate to be used by Him—people who are not content to be average, but who want to be mightily used of God.

While I was preaching this message, about three-quarters of the way through Heidi left her seat, came to the altar and began to pray for God to touch her. I remember seeing Heidi praying there. She looked up at me with tears streaming down her face. Immediately I was aware of a strong impression to speak the following prophetic word to her: "Heidi, God wants to know, do you want the nation of Mozambique?" I did not try to figure out the word; I just gave it.

Heidi answered with a strong voice, "Yes!"

Then I said, "God is going to give you the nation of Mozambique. You are going to see the dumb speak, the lame walk, the blind see and the dead be raised."

Immediately God backed up this prophetic word with His mighty power and presence. The power of God came on Heidi with such force and intensity that she was rendered paralyzed from the neck down for a short period of time. She experienced heat, electricity, laughter and crying and thought she might die from the power. This lasted for seven days and nights. This was the most powerful experience of the Spirit that Heidi had ever had in her life. It was the most intense and longest in duration, and it produced the greatest fruit.

What came out of this impartation is a saga so remarkable that it is perhaps the most phenomenal harvest of souls in our present day. Heidi and Rolland's stories of miracles, divine appointments, provision, heroism and heartrending experiences could be straight from the book of Acts. They prove that Jesus Christ is indeed the same yesterday, today and forever! Through the Bakers, God has birthed a miraculous church-planting movement that now encompasses over ten thousand churches in ten nations, as well as over a million salvations.

Fruit for the Kingdom

It is important to be aware that receiving a prophetic word, as Heidi did, does not mean everything will suddenly become easy. More often, the prophetic word is what God uses to strengthen us during the difficult times that are soon to follow. I have noticed that there is often a relationship between the intensity of an experience with God and the degree of difficulty a person will face in fulfilling the call of God on his or her life. We must learn how to stand on the promises of the prophetic word. I will explore this concept more fully in chapter 7, "Radical Obedience."

Another thing to note is that although the Bakers received their impartations over a period of time, it does not always work that way. God will sometimes move quickly. He works with each of us in just the way we need to best equip us to bring about much fruit for His Kingdom.

The following testimonies from pastors, missionaries and laypersons give some understanding of how an impartation can change lives—both the lives of the people receiving the impartation and the lives of all those they will touch as a result. The information in these pages came through interviews I did directly with these people or through letters and emails they wrote to me about their impartation experiences. As you will see, each experience is as unique as the person receiving it, yet the similarity is that every one of these times of impartation produced fruit for the Kingdom.

Marcelo Casagrande

In 2003 I received an invitation to attend some revival meetings that were being held at Pastor Daniel Marins's Four Square church in São Paulo, Brazil. [Note: These were part of a Global Awakening conference. Daniel Marin was the president of the Four Square denomination in the state of São Paulo, so about twelve hundred pastors and their spouses were present.]

I confess that when I arrived at the church, I was annoyed. I found it all very strange—people were worshiping

God in a frantic way, shaking and swaying. Some were lying on the floor and rolling from side to side. I saw all of that and thought to myself, **Do they really need all that to talk to God, or to feel His presence?** You see, I was the pastor of a charismatic Baptist Church and we believed in the baptism of the Holy Spirit and in tongues, but still, the things I saw at the meetings were too much for my understanding.

Suddenly, as I was judging all that I saw, my leg started to shake without anyone touching me. I did not understand anything about that kind of revival and I wanted my leg to stop doing that, but I could not stop it. I had some people from my church along whom I had brought to the meetings, and I thought, **What are my people going to think if they see my leg shaking like that?**

In an attempt to stop my leg from shaking, I held it with my hand really tightly. But instead of stopping the leg, it got worse because then my hand also started to shake. I looked over my shoulder to see if my people were seeing this, and then my arm and shoulder started to shake. Before I could understand what was going on, I felt myself on the ground with my whole body shaking, impacted by a wonderful presence of God. I stayed there on the floor for hours, having a visitation from God.

After the meeting was over, I managed to get up with some help. I got to my car but could not drive home because my legs were still shaking so badly, so I asked a member of my church to drive my car and take me home. I heard that there would be some training at the church the next morning, so I went back for it. At that point, I didn't care anymore about what people thought—I knew it was God, and I wanted more.

When I got to the training, though, I remember thinking, **Why do they teach about healing? There's nothing to teach! God heals whomever He wants to heal. We just pray, and if it is His will, He will heal. There's nothing for me to learn here.** I could not have been more wrong! I learned more about healing in that one morning than in all my years of training to become a pastor.

On the third night of the conference, Randy taught on impartation. Afterward, he began to pray for the presence of God to touch people. I remember him saying, "All the people who are shaking, feeling electricity, heat, energy or some manifestation of God's presence, please come forward and stretch your hands forward with palms up, as if you're going to receive a gift, because the Father will give you gifts this evening."

Many people went to the front, including me. I was shaking intensely. Randy came up and asked me if I had rubbed some kind of oil on my hands. I told him that I had not, but once he mentioned it, I could also see that the palms of my hands were covered with a large amount of oil, so much that it was dripping to the floor. I told him that I hadn't put anything on my hands and that such a thing had never happened to me before.

Randy looked at me and said, "The miracle anointing is upon this pastor!" When he said this he breathed on me, and the anointing fell on me so hard that I flew backward about ten feet. I knocked a bunch of people to the ground with me as I touched them with my anointed hands, and I got stuck on the floor for a couple of hours, shaking and impacted by the power of God being released on my life.

Again that night I could not drive my car, so a friend drove me home. When I got there, all I could do for the next three days was cry. I cried for three days and three nights straight. There came a time when I had no more tears, but I could not stop crying because of the presence of God. During these three days and nights I ate nothing. My wife tried to convince me to eat some food, but I could not eat or drink at all; I could only cry. She asked me why I was crying so much, and I told her it was because of God's presence. I realized later that during that time God was healing me of a wound that I had deep down in my soul. The first miracle the Lord did in my life was in my heart. He was getting me ready for something big, but I had no idea of how big it would be.

After the third day of crying, I got up very hungry in the afternoon and went to a bakery near my house. On the way there, I got a word of knowledge for healing. I knew it was a word of knowledge because I had learned about it during the training that Randy had given us. When I arrived at the bakery, I stayed connected with the Holy Spirit to find out whom the word of knowledge was for. When I went to the cashier to pay for my pastries, I felt that the word was for a lady standing in the line. I walked up to her and asked if by chance she had a pain in her right shoulder.

She looked at me wide-eyed and asked, "How do you know that?"

I told her. "I'm a Christian, and sometimes Jesus tells me things He wants to heal for people."

She then told me she was in terrible pain in her right shoulder. She could not lift it at all due to the pain.

I told her that when God gives a word of knowledge, He wants to heal, and I asked if I could pray for her. She said sure, so I placed my hands on her shoulder.

Startled, the lady said, "Oh, do you mean now? Here at the bakery? Don't I have to come to church or something?"

"Yes, now," I told her. "God can heal you right here at the bakery. You don't have to go to church. I will pray for you with my voice down low and my eyes open; no one will even notice that I'm praying for you."

Then she replied, "Okay then."

I placed my hands on her shoulder and prayed under my breath, saying, "Holy Spirit, come; in the name of Jesus, shoulder, be healed." I finished this short prayer, which I had learned from Randy's teaching, and asked her if she felt any better.

She tried to move her arm, and to her surprise—and to my surprise, as well—she was totally healed! She could now lift her arm and touch her hair, something she could not have done at all before. She marveled and glorified God for her healing, and I instructed her to look for a church near her home to attend. I told her to tell everyone about what God had done for her. She said she would and thanked me, crying.

From that day onward, the Lord continued to use me in several places. Wherever I went, He gave me words of knowledge and I would pray for people who would get healed. It happened at the butcher's, at the supermarket and in many other places.

On the next Sunday after my visitation and impartation from Randy, I started to preach as I always did, but there was something different about me. God's presence was evident in my life. At a certain time during worship, I quickly shared my recent experience and invited people to come forward to receive prayer for healing. I had about five hundred people in my church, and most of them came to the front. I came down from the pulpit to minister to people with the laying on of hands. When I raised my hands to pray for them, they began to fall under the power of God, filled with the Holy Spirit. Some were shaking, some were laughing and some were being baptized in the Holy Ghost.

Even though I didn't get to pray for them directly, a large number of people who were sick were healed instantly. One woman had an illness in her stomach, a terrible infection that doctors could not heal. She spent a week sick at home and fifteen days in the hospital, but it amounted to nothing. She came up for prayer that morning, and the anointing was so strong that she fell on the floor, and then people saw a three-inch-long maggot crawl out of her nose. She was instantly and completely healed. She was not a Christian and had been involved with witch doctors, but that morning she got her healing and gave her life to the Lord.

Soon after that, I began to receive invitations to preach in several regions in Brazil. I went to all the places where the Lord led me, and in all the meetings God healed a large number of people. In July 2011, I was in a large meeting with Randy Clark again here in Brazil. Randy's spiritual son, Ed Rocha, prayed for me. I fell to the ground, and I felt terrible and wonderful crunches in my belly. Ed got down on his knees beside me, took off his watch and placed it on my wrist, saying, "A new season is being opened up by the Lord in your ministry. A new time will arrive and it has already begun. You will be invited to minister all over South America, and the level of your anointing will increase."

At that point I had not yet left Brazil to minister. Sure enough, not long after that night I got invitations to preach in Uruguay, Paraguay and Argentina. It has been a year since Ed gave me that word, and since then, I have been to all the countries in South America to preach about the power of God to heal. I have ministered to literally thousands of people who have been touched by the healing power of Jesus. I have prayed and seen over eighty blind people recover their vision, over seventy deaf people receive their hearing, over thirty dumb start to speak and over sixty lame walk. Many other signs are manifested during my meetings. Gold teeth, pins, screws and metal rods in people's bodies have turned into bone or disappeared, and many people have recovered the ability to move a limb that they could not move before due to the metal. You can watch hundreds of such video testimonies on YouTube under my name, Marcelo Casagrande. I thank the Lord and glorify His name for the life of Randy Clark, whom God used to forever change my life and ministry.

Mike Kaylor
Fort Lauderdale, Florida

To say that I was disillusioned with my life and ministry would be an understatement. After thirty years in ministry and five "movements," I was desperate for the reality of the presence of God.

At a meeting in Toronto with Randy, my wife had been healed of a debilitating pain no doctors could explain in the upper part of her back and shoulders. I had heard of the tremendous outpouring of power and impartation happening on Randy's ministry trips, and I knew that if my hunger was to be addressed, I would need to go where heaven seemed to be opened. As a result, I made my first ministry trip to Brazil with Randy. One of the wonderful blessings of being on the trip was the fact that there was a special time set aside to pray for impartation for the team. As I stood waiting for my time to be prayed for, my mind raced with excitement and wonder as I saw people respond to the prayer with a myriad of reactions. I thought to myself, **What if I am the only one in the room that nothing happens to?**

Before I could finish that thought, Randy was standing in front of me. He began to pray as he laid his hand on my forehead. I suddenly found myself on my knees, with uncontrollable shaking and my arms flailing all over the place. As scary as it was, I did not want to stop something God was doing. I said, "Lord, let it come."

A heat started on the inside of me until it consumed my whole body from head to toe. I felt as though I were on fire! As this impartation continued, I heard the Lord say, "You wanted it—you've got it!"

I felt a strange tingling sensation going into my forehead. It was as if an angel placed something inside there. This happened three times. I began to receive an understanding about the realm of the angelic and the angels that had been assigned to me. The impartation continued into the next night, when I had to be carried out of the meeting because I was unable to stand, much less walk.

After this impartation, I began to notice a difference during ministry time. Once, as I prayed for a young girl, I felt a gust of wind come over me in a room that was totally enclosed. My translator said she thought that the Lord was making me sensitive to the angelic. Another time, as I was praying for a young man I put my hand on his forehead. To my surprise, he literally flew back eight feet in the air. The next person I prayed for was a woman in need of healing. As I began to pray for her, she said that the area she needed healing in was becoming hot. She received her healing, and

I moved on to the next person, who told me the same exact thing. Heat was surrounding the area that needed healing! I knew then that something wonderful had been imparted to me. These things had never happened before.

After that time, when I would pray for impartation for others, many of them seemed to receive the same consuming fire of God. As John Wimber said, "Whatever you receive, go and give it away." I felt as if it were Christmas and I was going around giving away free gifts to anyone who would take them.

I fully believe that the impartation or download from heaven that was given to me was not because of anything that I did to attain it. It came in response to a deep hunger that brought me to a place where I could receive.

Pastor Silvio Galli
São Paulo, Brazil

I received impartation through several ministries, causing a radical change in my life and great renewal. In 2001 Pastor Randy came to our church. As he prayed for me, I could feel a big heat that came through the Holy Ghost. It was a glorious state. After this impartation, my ministerial and personal life was transformed. Today I have the intense presence of God's glory in my life, and through His grace I have imparted this same anointing to other people.

In the beginning, great resistance came from my family and church. When God started to move among us, things got out of control. Some people thought that what was going on was emotional or that we were exaggerating. Others thought that it was just momentary. After a while, people started to see our transformation. Soon they saw that it was not emotion, but something that came from God.

Pastor Randy Clark has been with us several times now. The first time in 2001, our church was traditional and we had around 350 people. When Randy came for the second time, we already had moved and we had around 1,200 people. The third time we had 3,000 people, and by the fourth time, in 2009, the church had grown to over 9,000. In 2010 we started 23 more churches out of this mother church. I know that this anointing came to bring other anointings, like the anointing to conquer the city, the multitudes and to grow the churches.

The anointing has a price. After the revival in our church, we needed to change some things in our doctrine. The anointing brought us many revelations. We have become one church that is multiplying. By 2020 we will open 200 new churches.

══ Anglican Father Bob Jepsen ══
Oceanside, California

I was ordained a priest in 1972 and began to experience a deep desire for greater intimacy with God and a desire to be filled with the Spirit and to receive the supernatural gifts. Fast-forward several years to a Rodney Howard-Browne conference called Abiding Place, at which I received an impartation. I believe it was in 1998. When Randy spoke at that conference, I received tremendous encouragement. I also caught the mission virus from him and ended up in Brazil. I was blown away at the meetings in Curitiba and Recife, Brazil. As I prayed for hundreds, I witnessed healings and signs and wonders. God used me to transfer the anointing to many others. Almost everyone I touched reported back that all their pain had left their bodies.

One night in Recife when Randy prayed over the team, I went down. While lying on the floor of the Anglican cathedral we were in, I believe God spoke to me and said I was to take teams to South America wherever He opened doors. In July 2003, my wife, our son, Peter, and I spent three weeks in Arequipa, Peru. I taught and trained nine seminary students and the pastor of the Anglican church to pray for healing. We planned a healing service, and fifty persons attended. Several were healed physically.

We had similar experiences at youth conferences and women's prisons and in Uganda in 2001. In Kisoro, I taught thirty Anglican pastors on the healing ministry, and for five days I was part of a team of sixteen Anglican and Pentecostal prayer warriors. This was my introduction to deliverance—big time. One Muslim man came to me for prayer. He told me, "There is a power in my head, and this power tried to cast me in the fire."

My response, what the Holy Spirit told me to say, was, "It's a demon that is trying to cast you into the fire, and only Jesus can get rid of the demon."

The man replied, "I want to accept Jesus."

Perhaps the greatest miracle I saw was deafness healed when I prayed for an older woman. She exclaimed to me, "Something popped in my ears and now they are fine!"

It is exciting for me to see how God has used Randy to set this very ordinary, very broken Anglican priest on fire for missions. In 2006 I led two ministry teams to Bolivia. I am so excited to live to see this day of revival and to be a part of this move of God shaking the nations (see Isaiah 64).

══ Johan Escoto ══

South America/Southwestern U.S.*

I received the baptism in the Holy Spirit as I was praying one day on my own. During that time, I received the call to minister. In 1991 I began a church under a larger ministry. When Randy Clark came to my country in 1996 and was visiting our ministry's churches, I received a word from the Lord through him. A friend wrote the prophecy down for me that day, and I still carry it with me. What my friend wrote is, "God has given you a unique or specific anointing that will have great impact. He will send you to the U.S. and many countries, as well as Canada, with signs and wonders. You will be a prophet of fire."

That was the beginning of a 20-day visitation from the Lord for me. An angel came with a torch of fire in his hand and put it in my hand. Then the angel made me swallow the torch. It burned my mouth and throat. When it reached my stomach, it caused an explosion in which I screamed and screamed. Then I could not walk for 22 days without being slain in the Spirit when I tried to get up.

Every little sin was magnified a thousand times. I would spend nights crying in God's presence. And people would have to hold me up to preach. Then everyone in the church would fall out or laugh and laugh. In the first meeting after the impartation I received, a woman had her arm in a cast, eaten away with bone cancer, and she was totally healed.

Many miracles, signs and wonders have continued happening since my impartation. Through my ministry, I now travel throughout the United States and around the world to bring the message of the saving, healing, transforming power of Jesus Christ and a fresh impartation of the fire of His presence.

*Name and identifying details have been changed.

Teresa Seputis
California

I had been a Christian for many years, having accepted Jesus as my Savior at the age of fourteen, but no one told me that Jesus had to be Lord (e.g., boss) of my life. As a result, my early Christian experience was not very successful or powerful, and I never developed a deep and intimate relationship with God. That is why I ended up backsliding in my late twenties for four or five years.

Shortly after I was married, though, I started feeling hungry for God. I began to fast, and my devotions and prayer time came alive. I enrolled at Fuller Theological Seminary so I could go into full-time ministry. I began to have prophetic knowledge of people's needs, but I had never heard of the prophetic gift and did not know what was happening.

In April 1994 I got an email about some amazing meetings in San Francisco where God was showing up in unusual ways. I went, received prayer and had an incredibly powerful encounter with God. My body began to shake, which lasted three hours. During that time, God kept telling me to trust Him. I continued to attend the meetings, and God met me powerfully each time. He began doing inner healing in me, and I began to feel loved and also able to love others with the love of Christ.

After this I began flying to Toronto, where Randy prayed for me several times at the revival. Every time he prayed for me, a passion for missions would burn in my soul. Randy came to minister in my home church in August 1994, and during these meetings I again experienced the tangible presence of God.

In 1995 and 1997 I went with Randy and a team to Moscow. On both of these trips, I saw God do amazing miracles when I prayed for people. I saw deaf ears open, semicrippled people walk and one instance when God grew back missing body parts. There was a lady who had been in a fire, and her kneecaps were burned off. When I prayed for her, God gave her new kneecaps! The thing that I took back from the second trip was that God really **will** heal the sick through me!

In June 2001, I started a healing school where people learned to pray for the sick and see people get healed. I am convinced that God wants everyone in the Body of Christ to be able to pray for and heal the sick.

In 2002 I was laid off from my job, five days before leaving on a trip to Brazil with Randy. Significant things happened to me on that trip. It was an incredible time where I saw the power and anointing of God in healing as never before. I felt that it was a foretaste of what to expect from God in terms of healing ministry. When I got home from Belém, I knew that God was taking me out of secular employment to live by faith and work full-time for Him.

I cannot help but think of Randy as a spiritual father since God used him to impart into me and to launch me into ministry. Randy also helped me gain enough boldness and confidence in the Lord to be able to conduct healing meetings in many different countries around the world.

[Note: After returning from the Russia trips, Teresa saw her ministry begin to grow from very humble beginnings into an interactive Internet training school for intercession and prophecy called GodSpeak International. Thousands of students have participated in the school, which is still active today. Many have been launched into their own powerful ministries through it.]

Dayoung Kimn
China

It was 1995 when I first met Randy Clark at a meeting in Langley, British Columbia. At the end of the meeting, he invited people to receive prayer. At that time, my ministry was in the beginning stage in China. I visited the underground churches there and trained them.

As I approached the front stage Randy came down, and I ran into him and asked for prayer. He prayed a very interesting prayer. This is how I remember it: "I pray for this man who is ministering to churches in China. Holy Spirit, fill him up! I pray and impart all of my spiritual inheritance through the prayer I have received from Benny Hinn, John Wimber . . ."

I do not remember the names of all the people Randy mentioned, but I felt very good and blessed. The following week, I was on my way to China. As I was leading one of the meetings there, I told the leaders I was going to pray for all of them to do more of what Jesus promised we all could do. I invited the Holy Spirit to touch them. I did not lay hands on anyone, but the Holy Spirit moved among these leaders. Many told me that they felt something and that they were feeling heat in their bodies.

One of the elderly ladies in her seventies, who served in the Chinese Red Army, later told me that she was healed from severe arthritis. She had been unable to sleep well for forty years, she said. After the meeting, she got up to help her daughter work. After that, she went out ministering to the neighbors and brought them to the Lord. Someone told me that she brought about seventy people to the Lord. I also found out that many of the leaders whom I prayed with are pioneering more churches than ever and are winning many souls to the Lord.

This made me think about what impartation is all about. Because of my experiences, I seriously meditated on the word **impartation**. In the year 2000, I began the ministry called Impartation Ministries International, which is still going strong today.

Dr. Denise Meisburg
Jacksonville, Florida

It all started back when I was attending a conference with my friend Cheryl Schang. Cheryl had seriously damaged knees that no surgery or therapy could help. The medical professionals predicted her mobility would be severely impaired for the rest of her life. She believed in healing and had been prayed for many times, but was still waiting.

When our conference was over, we noticed that some other meeting was going on in the facility next door. We went over to check it out. Randy Clark was just finishing a message and leaving the stage to walk around and pray for people. As Cheryl came through the door, Randy suddenly said, "Somebody is getting their knee healed." Randy's ministry team prayed for Cheryl and received accurate words of knowledge about other medical conditions that she had, but they were not praying for her knees. She had a heart condition and it was healed, but not her knees!

Randy was still asking, "Who's got the knee problem?" We cut through the crowd and got close enough for Cheryl to tell him, "It's me."

Randy never touched Cheryl. Instead, he got on his knees and prayed very simply as he was bowed before her, "Jesus, I'm just the colt of the donkey you ride on." (By that he meant that the healing power was not his, but was from the Spirit. Randy saw himself as the donkey colt Jesus rode on Palm Sunday, simply a servant, and he wanted all praise to go to the Lord for whatever happened.)

As Randy prayed that prayer, I felt a tangible wind blow across us. Cheryl was instantly healed. She started jumping and screaming, rejoicing and praising Jesus.

In the midst of that, Randy turned to me and said, "And you—you will be involved in Jewish evangelism in Russia and the Ukraine regions."

Randy had never met me and did not know I was Jewish. His prophetic word was a pivotal event in my life. It changed my self-perception in regard to my calling beyond that of a wife, mother and nurse. It encouraged me to become equipped and ready. The prophetic word makes room for what God wants to do, if you will believe it and act on it. I believe God has led me to be diligent and responsible to that word.

In 2003 I finished a doctorate degree in counseling so that I could get out into the secular marketplace. In 2004 my husband and I went to the Catch the Fire conference in Toronto. We specifically went there from Jacksonville, Florida, in order to thank Randy for his impact on my life the first time he had prayed for me, almost five years before. As I shared my testimony, he prophesied over me again, this time saying I was to be involved in national Jewish evangelism.

Randy did not know that my husband and I were just getting started with teaching the HaYesod program, which is basically a Jewish roots class for Gentiles. But his prophecies had a tremendous impact in helping me take hold of God's calling, exercise the faith to walk in it and have the motivation to prepare myself for its outworking. I have been privileged to see what I believe is only the beginning of a great last-days outpouring of God's glory in the world. But ministering in His power is not just about getting a prophecy or an impartation. It is about knowing His heart. You cannot use His power unless you know His heart! And that takes time. No prophecy or impartation can take the place of time with Jesus. Do you want to see His glory? Take the time to get to know Him!

Bearing Fruit for the Kingdom

Each person's story told in the preceding pages bears out the fruit of impartation. Through the impartations they received, each person was changed, empowered and directed. They then responded by walking in and fulfilling their God-given destinies. What I hope that you take away from these amazing stories is that God can take ordinary people, touch them through impartation and reach the world. That could mean *you*! In chapter 8 ahead, called "Clothed with Power: Nobody Is Safe," I will talk more about exactly that—how nobody is safe when the presence of God comes in power.

In the next chapter, though, I want to highlight an important kind of impartation—an impartation to "see" into the spiritual realm. This is a key to greater miracles and more healings in one's ministry or life. I myself am asking, seeking and knocking for this impartation.

5

Impartation to See

The Bible records several people *seeing* into the spiritual realm. Numbers 22:31 records that Balaam's eyes were opened to see. "Then the LORD opened the eyes of Balaam, and he saw the angel of the LORD standing in the way with his drawn sword in his hand; and he bowed all the way to the ground" (NASB). David's eyes were also opened to see the angelic in 2 Samuel 24:17. "Then David spoke to the LORD when he saw the angel who was striking down the people" (NASB). And in 2 Kings 2:9, Elijah tells Elisha, "Ask what I shall do for you before I am taken from you." Elisha responds, "Please, let a double portion of your spirit be upon me" (NASB). On the occasion of receiving this double-portion anointing, Elisha saw what I believe were some of the heavenly host, the angels of God taking Elijah to heaven. The eyes of Gehazi, Elisha's servant, were opened in 2 Kings 6:17. "Elisha prayed and said, 'O LORD, I pray, open his eyes that he may see.' And the

LORD opened the servant's eyes and he saw; and behold, the mountain was full of horses and chariots of fire all around Elisha."

The New Testament also records events where people's eyes were opened to see into the spiritual realm and to see the angelic. John the Baptist's father, Zacharias, saw the angel who appeared to him. Jesus' mother, Mary, saw an angel who explained God's will for her. Mary Magdalene saw two angels near the tomb of Jesus. Peter saw the angel who delivered him from prison. Paul saw the angel who appeared during the terrible storm at sea to encourage him. On the Isle of Patmos John received the revelation of Jesus, which an angel interpreted to him. He saw the angel and fell down to worship, but the angel told him to worship God alone. (See Luke 1:11–12, 26–38; John 20:11–12; Acts 12:4–11; 27:23–24; Revelation 19:10.)

New Testament professor James D. G. Dunn notes in his book *Jesus and the Spirit: A Study of the Religious and Charismatic Experience of Jesus and the First Christians as Reflected in the New Testament* (Westminster Press, 1975) that visions and angelic visitations were one of three primary sources for authority in the lives of the earliest Christian communities. With the canon of Scripture, we have the benefit of an objective guide to the discernment of any experience. Nevertheless, it is important to note how God has continued, throughout history, to communicate with His people through the means of supernatural visitation.

The prophecy I received on January 19, 1994, the night before I went to Toronto for the first time, changed my life. It gave me faith to expect a mighty outpouring of God, more than I had ever seen before in my life. However, months later

I realized I had neither appropriated nor recognized all that had been given to me through this prophecy. I had missed the "seeing" part of the prophecy. As I said in chapter 2, the prophetic word was, "Test Me now. Test Me now. Test Me now. Do not be afraid. I will back you up! *I want your eyes to be opened to see into the heavenlies My resources for you, just as Elisha prayed for Gehazi's eyes to be opened.* And do not become anxious, because when you become anxious, you can't hear Me" (emphasis added).

I realized later that I had been powerfully impacted by all the prophecy except the part about my eyes being opened. Then, for about two years, I began to get other significant prophecies that had the same theme I had overlooked: "God wants you to see!" The most significant word I received came to me on October 15, 1996, through the powerful, anointed servant of God Ruth Heflin. I did not know who Ruth Heflin was at the time, but she came to Philadelphia where I was ministering for thirty days to give me a word from the Lord she had received for me in Jerusalem. Here's a portion of the prophetic word she gave me at Deliverance Evangelistic Church in Philadelphia (emphasis added):

> . . . For again and again thou shalt stand upon this platform and thou shalt begin to see in new realms of the Spirit; *for I remove every scale from thine eye and thou shalt see those things that thou hast longed to see*; thou shalt see that which is afar and that which is near. Thou shalt see that which is hidden and that which is revealed. Thou shalt see in measures beyond any that thou hast experienced until this time. For it shall be the anointing of the seer that shall come greatly upon thee and *thou shalt see and describe that which thou seest and even as thou proclaimest it, so shall the miracles come forth, saith the Lord.*

. . . For the seeing shall cause a new faith to be brought forth; a greater measure of faith than that which thou hast known; a greater measure of faith than that which thou hast walked in; a greater measure of faith than that which thou hast witnessed; *thou shalt see it in the heavenlies and thou shall speak it forth and so shall it be.*

. . . This is the day, the day of the Lord. This is the day, the day of the Lord. This is the hour, the hour of visitation. This is the time, the time of manifestation; the manifestation of My Spirit, the manifestation of My power, the manifestation of My glory, the manifestation yea, of My mighty arm made bare with signs and wonders and miracles, signs and wonders—miracles—healings, yea a healing stream that shall flow to the north, the south, the east and west, and shall encompass all nations, a mighty healing stream, yea a mighty healing stream . . .

Because I had good friends who had prophetic gifts and who experienced open visions, my view of what it meant to see into the spiritual was somewhat skewed. The prophet Bob Jones told me by telephone that I did see, but that my seeing came in the form of a "knowing" so strong that I would be moved to declare things in meetings and then see them happen. I am glad for this sense of seeing that I do have, though I would also like to see open visions or even strong mental pictures.

Faith is built up by seeing. It is this built-up faith that then causes us to have the courage to speak out what we believe God is about to do in a meeting. A strategic passage for my understanding of moving in the power of the Spirit and seeing miracles is 2 Corinthians 4:13: "It is written: 'I believed; therefore I have spoken.' With that same spirit of faith we also believe and therefore speak." I think the spirit of faith Paul refers to here is related to understanding what God is doing in the moment. This risk-taking faith comes from a sense of knowing through some revelational gift or experience from God. The greater the faith, the more powerful the anointing will be on a meeting for healing, deliverance and miracles.

Gary Oates

One of my very good friends, Gary Oates, who has been in the ministry for more than forty years, has accompanied me on more than one trip to Brazil. He was so hungry for a touch of God, an impartation from God. In time, he became just as hungry for an impartation to see as Jesus sees. For those who want to do what the Father is doing, the gift of "seeing" is a gift to earnestly desire. Gary wanted his eyes opened to see into the spiritual realm. Here are excerpts from Gary's story as he relates his experiences in Brazil:

> The night of the first meeting (in September 2000), Randy spoke briefly about the value of impartation. Then he lined up all the pastors and came down the line, praying for impartation for each person. When he stood in front of me, the power of God hit me and I went down.
>
> At the meeting later that night, Randy called up the pastors on the team to pray over the Brazilian pastors. I went up to offer my prayers. A Brazilian pastor and his wife came and stood in front of me. When I reached over to pray for them, the power of God hit them and they went flying backward. They literally skidded across the floor.
>
> The next person I prayed for was an older man. He seemed to have no flexibility or mobility in his legs and could barely walk. I prayed for his legs, and the power of God came down upon him and he was totally healed. Later I prayed for another

man in the latter stages of emphysema and also with a hearing problem. God immediately healed the man's lungs, and he no longer needed a hearing aid.

In 2001 I went on another Global Awakening trip with Randy to Brazil. Randy prayed for impartation again, and I saw an even greater increase in anointing for healing, creative miracles and a sense of the presence of God.

When a third Global trip came about for June 2002, my wife, Kathi, came with me. That 2002 trip to Brazil changed our lives. Our church appeared as if it were coming apart at the seams. (Several key families had to leave our church and community due to job transfers to other cities at about that time.) I was desperate; I had to have a touch from God myself. I prayed, "Lord, I want to see beyond the natural. I want to see angels. I want to see into the realm of the Spirit."

My eyes were opened to see beyond the natural realm into the realm of the Spirit, including seeing the ministry of angels. I had a dramatic encounter with the Lord—being caught up into His presence—where I saw the Lord Jesus while out of my body. For about an hour, I lay mute on the floor.

[Note: This experience may have been similar to what the apostle Paul describes in 2 Corinthians 12:2, "Whether it was in the body or out of the body I do not know—God knows."]

The next night, before the meeting began, a man laid his hand on my left shoulder. The power of God suddenly surged through me, and I fell like a dead man. Again, I couldn't move. I cried out, "God, I want more of You! I want more of You! I want more of You!"

Instantly I was transported into a heavenly setting, where Jesus was standing on the right side of a throne with a scepter in His hand. I saw the glory of God like I had never seen it before, and I found myself crying out, "God, forgive me . . . forgive me!"

Randy later called me to the platform to explain what had happened to me. Since I was unable to speak, Kathi took the microphone and explained a little bit. As she did, the Spirit of God fell in that place. People began crying out; others were falling on their faces in repentance. God was doing a spontaneous, yet miraculous work in that church.

Randy instructed the team members to lift my hands and lay them on each pastor's head. As soon as my hands touched a pastor's head, he went out in the Spirit. Later, when I was finally able to stand up, I began praying for people. A long line formed, and almost everybody I prayed for indicated that they were healed.

On that same trip to Brazil, although she had gone reluctantly, Kathi had a vision of being taken before God's throne in heaven. Within days, she was launched into a new realm of prophetic utterances and seeing angels as well. Our lives would never be the same again.

There is little doubt that impartation played a key role in the experiences Kathi and I have had. Because of the impartations we have received, our lives and ministry have been radically transformed.

Revelational Gifts and Seeing

Through the multiple examples I have listed from Scripture, and through testimonies like the one I just shared from Pastor Gary Oates, it is clear that God gives revelatory gifts that may allow someone to literally "see" into the spiritual realm. However, there is also a sense in Scripture in which seeing is understood as perceiving. Repeatedly, Jesus accuses His detracting observers of having eyes to see, but seeing not. In that context, the seeing referred to is obviously an understanding of the significance of what God was doing through Jesus' works. It refers to an awareness of the purposes of God in the moment or situation. These understandings are often received through revelational gifts such as prophecy, words of knowledge, words of wisdom or discerning of spirits.

In Jesus' Upper Room discourse, there is a clear connection between revelation given by the Holy Spirit and doing the supernatural works of God. In John 14:10–14, Jesus tells the disciples the Father is in Him and He is in the Father. He tells them it is the Father living in Him who is doing the works and giving Him the very words to say. Then Jesus tells the disciples that anyone who has faith in Him will do what He has been doing. And, this is *because* Jesus was going to the Father. This is an obvious reference to His crucifixion, resurrection and ascension to His Father in heaven. This was necessary for the outpouring of the Holy Spirit (see also John 7:37–39). It will be this new role of the Holy Spirit, under the New Covenant, that will make the "even greater things than these" that believers will do possible (John 14:12). The reason Jesus gave for doing "whatever you ask in my name" was "so that the Son might bring glory to the Father" (verse 13). That was the reason Jesus told us, "You may ask me for anything in my name, and I will do it" (verse 14).

But if you ask how one begins to do these "greater things," the answer starts in John 14:15, where it is rooted in love for Jesus. This love manifests in obedience to His commands. On this condition, Jesus asks the Father to send us the "Paraclete," another Counselor. Jesus told the disciples that this other Counselor, the Holy Spirit, was already dwelling with them—but would be in them (see verse 17). The Holy Spirit's unity with Jesus is like that of Jesus' unity with the Father— so much so that to receive the Holy Spirit is to receive Jesus. Jesus literally tells the disciples in verse 18, "I will come to you."

Jesus then gives us a key to receiving revelation—"seeing" comes from receiving the "all-seeing One" on a continual basis. Revelation comes out of intimacy, and intimacy is connected to love manifesting itself through obedience. Jesus indicates that the one who obeys in love will be loved and will receive a revelation of Jesus. "Whoever has my commands and obeys them, he is the one who loves me. He who loves me will be loved by my Father, and I too will love him and *show myself to him*" (John 14:21, emphasis added).

Out of the intimacy that comes from obeying and remaining in Jesus the vine, we the branches will bear "much fruit" (John 15:5). It is out of this abiding relationship that we, not just the twelve disciples, are enabled to bear much fruit. "If you remain in me and my words remain in you, ask whatever you wish, and it will be given you" (verse 7).

Again, the result of our fruitfulness is the "Father's glory." In bearing much fruit, we are "showing" ourselves to be Jesus' disciples (verse 8). I believe that as we receive revelations from Jesus, these revelations produce belief so strong that we have courage to speak. Our speaking in faith produces the "much fruit" that reveals we are disciples of Jesus. This is how the words of Paul in 2 Corinthians 4:13 and Jesus' words in John chapters 14–16 particularly fit together. This understanding is made clearer in John 15:14–16:

> You are my friends if you do what I command. I no longer call you servants, because a servant does not know his master's business. Instead, I have called you friends, for everything that I have learned from my Father I have made known to you. You did not choose me, but I chose you and appointed you to go and bear fruit—fruit that will last.

Revelation produces fruit because it produces faith. Revelation is referred to here in the phrase "everything that I have learned from my Father I have *made known to you*" (emphasis added). This revelation comes out of the relationship of sonship and love revealed through knowledge of His Word and obedience to it.

Jesus says more about the promise of revelation in John 16:12–15 (emphasis added):

> I have much more to say to you, more than you can now bear. But when he, the Spirit of truth, comes, he will guide you into all truth. He will not speak on his own; he will speak only what he hears, and he *will tell you what is yet to come. He will bring glory to me by taking from what is mine and making it known to you.* All that belongs to the Father is mine. That is why I said the Spirit will take from what is mine and *make it known to you.*

If seeing in the sense of perceiving is key to producing much fruit, then it behooves all of us to desire to see better into the spiritual realm and into spiritual truths. I have now been in ministry for over 41 years, and I have discussed this with others who likewise have been in ministry for more than 40 years. They report that when they were able to know by seeing in the sense of perceiving, their faith exploded. Additionally, if there are some who also begin to literally see into the spiritual realm through a spiritual grace or gift, would it not then be the better part of wisdom to desire this literal seeing, while at the same time being grateful for any of the various ways God allows us to see by perceiving?

In trying to make this clearer, let me say that I now see/perceive the desire of God during a meeting by "feeling" in my body the conditions He wants to heal—this is how the gift of word of knowledge most often works in me. I also "know" the direction of God for a situation through impressions in my mind. I know that greater certainty produces even greater faith, and the greater the clarity, the greater the certainty.

I invite you to hunger and thirst with me for greater intimacy and for the humility to cry out for greater revelation. I can no longer be satisfied by learning more about Jesus. I now know it is possible to hear His voice audibly, to be taken into Isaiah 6 experiences today and, as John did in the beginning of the book of Revelation, to see Him in His exalted state. And, though this is my greatest desire, I likewise desire to see into the Kingdom of God—both to see things from His point of view and to see heavenly beings interacting with us on our behalf. I believe impartations for this ability, this grace to see in the ways I have talked about, are being transferred today. I hope to receive more of them myself.

PART 3

Evangelism
and Missions
The Power Factor

But you will receive power when the Holy Spirit comes on you; and you will be my witnesses in Jerusalem, and in all Judea and Samaria, and to the ends of the earth.

~ *Acts 1:8*

My message and my preaching were not with wise and persuasive words, but with a demonstration of the Spirit's power, so that your faith might not rest on men's wisdom, but on God's power.

~ *1 Corinthians 2:4–5*

6

Why Impartations?
Why Signs and Wonders?

True Christianity hinges on a theology of presence—the presence of God. The Christian life is based on a personal relationship with the living God, whose ultimate desire is to be known by us as we are known by Him (see 1 Corinthians 13:12). He reveals His heart, His thoughts and His purposes to those who walk in friendship with Him. Though He is invisible, He can be felt, heard and seen, sometimes by manifest visitation, sometimes by effect, just as we see the effects of the wind, though not the wind itself.

If you take away the elements of experience and revelation, you are left with religion—perhaps an admirable system of ethics and rules, but not much of a relationship. All through the Bible, the ultimate authority on revelation, we see the various means by which God chooses to reveal Himself.

These include the working of miracles, healing, dreams and visions, the prophetic word and other manifestation gifts of the Spirit. Sadly, those who dismiss these vehicles of God's self-revelation, saying they have ceased, are dismissing much of what is most precious and dynamic about a relationship with God.

Our God has an incredible desire to reveal Himself. In Isaiah 65:1, the prophet Isaiah tells us that God reveals Himself even to those who are neither asking for nor seeking Him. Romans 1:20 says all of creation serves to reveal His eternal power and divine nature. The gospel of John tells us that the Holy Spirit is sent to believers to reveal the very plans and thoughts of God. David, writing by inspiration of the Holy Spirit, prayed often for the glory of God to be revealed among the nations. Throughout Scripture, God promises to "show" or "reveal" His glory (see John 1:14). Jesus came that we might see God's glory as "a light for revelation to the Gentiles and for glory to your people Israel" (Luke 2:32).

The Body of Christ is intended to further the revelation of God in this world (see 1 John 4:17). It should not surprise us, then, to see revival accompanied by demonstrations of the power and glory of God. Even the gifts and manifestations of the Holy Spirit pale in comparison to those times when God chooses to "rend the heavens and come down" in His glory. His glory produces many more healings and powerful impartations than any of His gifts.

This is entirely consistent with God's expressed desire to reveal Himself! Those who think God has quieted down over the years or has retreated behind the clouds until the return of Jesus really do not understand the passion God has for drawing people to Himself through the revelation of His glory.

What exactly do we mean by "God's glory"? Moses asked God, "Now show me your glory" (Exodus 33:18). Perhaps Moses expected God to shatter the heavens with lightning and thunder, or perhaps embellish upon the burning bush by setting the mountain on fire. Instead, God responded to Moses, "I will cause *all my goodness* to pass in front of you, and I will proclaim my name, the LORD, in your presence" (verse 19, emphasis added). Here God Himself defines His glory; it is His character and His nature as expressed in His names that constitute His glory. As He passed by Moses, He proclaimed His compassion, His grace, His abounding love, His willingness to forgive and His perfect justness.

How does God reveal His glory in the world? The Bible contains eighteen categories of instances where the glory of God is mentioned. By far, the largest category is miracles and healings, where God's glory is connected thirty times to a demonstration of His power through the working of signs, wonders and miracles. Based on this fact, we could say that the *main way* God reveals His glory is through signs, wonders and miracles.[1]

This puts a new perspective on what we are asking God to do when we sing, "Glorify Thy name, glorify Thy name, glorify Thy name in all the earth." We are actually asking God to work His mighty power in our midst. We are asking Him to reveal His nature as expressed in His covenantal name, *Jehovah Rapha*, the Lord our Healer. We are asking for a revelation of God's *goodness!* This is so important in a world where so many think of God as distant, uncaring, unfair, angry or just not there at all!

This also puts a new perspective on the phrase, "Don't touch His glory." Are we not in some way robbing God of His glory when we hold to a cessationist view of God's continued activity in this world?

The connection between God's glory and demonstrations of His power first occurred to me as I was reading the gospel of John. The connection is first made in John 2:11: "This, the first of his miraculous signs, Jesus performed at Cana in Galilee. He thus revealed his glory, and his disciples put their faith in him."

Jesus understood that the miracle of Lazarus's resurrection took place for God's glory: "When he heard this, Jesus said, 'This sickness will not end in death. No, it is for God's glory so that God's Son may be glorified through it'" (John 11:4). This passage teaches us that both the Father and the Son were glorified by this miracle. Jesus believed that in witnessing the resurrection of Lazarus, the disciples and the others present were actually seeing the glory of God. Then Jesus said, "Did I not tell you that if you believed, you would see the glory of God?" (John 11:40).

John noted in his gospel that though the Pharisees and scribes had witnessed the miracles of Jesus, they still did not believe. The Bible is clear that the main way God reveals His glory is through signs and wonders, healing and miracles. The only thing that comes close in comparison is the cloud by day and the fire by night in the Exodus. I am not talking about taking claim for what God did, of course, but that is not the only way we touch His glory. Both Paul and John use *glory* and *power* synonymously. We bring glory to God by bearing much fruit (see John 14–16). It is the Sovereign's will that we do what His Son did and even greater things—thus bringing Him glory.

I find it ironic that so many people express in their theology a great concern for the glory of God, yet they miss this aspect of sovereignty as revealed in God's Son. Jesus explicitly stated that God's will for us is to bring Him glory, and this emphasis was clearly related to doing the works Jesus Himself had been doing. This theme of the Father or the Son being glorified and their glory being revealed through signs and wonders is most clear in the Upper Room discourse of Jesus recorded in John chapters 14–16 and in the High Priestly prayer of Jesus in John 17. Jesus teaches that He will answer our prayers in His name so that by answering our prayers the *Father will be glorified*.

When the following scriptural texts are read in context, beyond a doubt the "greater things" reference pertains to doing acts of power, signs, wonders, healing and miracles. "Greater things than these [shall you do] because I go to the Father" in John 14:12 is clearly not a reference to moral ethics, but to charismatic acts done through charismatic gifts made possible by the future ministry of the Holy Spirit. John 14:13–14 continues, "And I will do whatever you ask in my name, so that the Son may bring *glory to the Father*. You may ask me for anything in my name, and I will do it" (emphasis added).

Jesus sees the Father's glory as in some way connected to our fruitfulness. In North America, there is much emphasis on the "fruit of the Spirit," but Jesus also spoke of fruit in the context of the powerful work of the Holy Spirit done through His disciples. "Fruit" is not limited to the Galatians 5 description (love, joy, peace . . .), but must be understood to include healings, deliverances and miracles. This is the nature of the fruit in John 15:8: "This is to my Father's glory, that you bear much fruit, showing yourselves to be my disciples."

The New Testament/Jewish concept of discipleship in Jesus' time was for the disciple to become like the master not only in his teaching, but in his life and living. Jon Ruthven, professor emeritus of Systematic and Practical Theology at Regent University School of Divinity, comments that Jesus continues to build His Church and advance His Kingdom through His disciples, and through their disciples after them, by answering their prayers and enabling them to truly be His disciples.[2]

When we consider how important the power to work miracles, healing, and deliverances was to Jesus' understanding to how both He and the Father were glorified, and when we consider Jesus' commissioning of the 12, 72, and through the apostles those who were to believe on their message, we cannot underestimate the priority Jesus placed on the ministry of the Kingdom's expansion through the words and works that He modeled for His disciples. The modeling was for them to understand the nature of the Kingdom of God. The Gospel of the Kingdom of God was not just to consist in talk, but also was to display power, as Paul says in 1 Corinthians 2:4–5: "My message and my preaching were not with wise and persuasive words, but with a demonstration of the Spirit's power, so that your faith might not rest on men's wisdom, but on God's power."

Let me back up this statement by quoting from the "Implications and Conclusions" section of Ruthven's book *On the Cessation of the Charismata*. Ruthven does an excellent job of capturing what I feel is the Father's heart for the Church, especially as expressed by the father to the elder brother in Jesus' parable of the Prodigal Son, where the father says, "My son, you are always with me, and everything I have is yours" (Luke 15:31).

The frequent failure to respond to God's commands to manifest the Kingdom of God in power is fully shared by most believers, "Charismatics" and non-Charismatics alike. Both groups shape their theology and consequent practice on the basis of their own experience–or lack of it–rather than on a fresh and radical (in its original sense of "return to the root") view of Scripture. The presence or absence of certain charismata in one's experience proves nothing at all about one's spiritual status or destiny.[3]

Here Ruthven quotes Matthew 7:21–22, "Not everyone who says to me, 'Lord, Lord,' will enter the kingdom of heaven, but only he who does the will of my Father who is in heaven. Many will say to me on that day, 'Lord, Lord, did we not prophesy in your name, and in your name drive out demons and perform many miracles?'" He goes on to say that neither charismatics nor "non" are more or less saved than the other. All are sinful, but justified by grace alone.

Nevertheless, Ruthven points out, the New Testament offers us patterns regarding how the Gospel is to be presented, received and lived out. "We must not attempt to reframe our failures into virtues," he says, "by allowing what the New Testament describes as 'unbelief' in and for the gifts of God, to be construed as having chosen 'the better way' of a 'stronger faith' without them."[4] In the case of the rabbis of Jesus' day, said Ruthven, their intellectualized biblical knowledge led to their cessationism and prompted Jesus to state, "You are in error because you do not know the Scriptures or the power of God" (Matthew 22:29).

Another important point Ruthven makes is that much divisiveness over the gifts of the Spirit today comes from a common premise held by both sides of the debate: evidentialism.

Conflict always follows when spiritual gifts are adduced as proofs of spiritual status or attainment, rather than used as tools for humble service for others. A core temptation for all of us is to "use spiritual knowledge and power to accredit one's independent and exalted religious status, instead of through them, rendering glory, obedience and service to God."[5] Ruthven maintains that although spiritual gifts are powerful weapons against the kingdom of darkness, they can wound and destroy the people of God when misapplied in evidentialist polemics. He concludes,

> The charismata, then, reflect the very nature of God, who does not share his glory with another. Similarly, God is a Spirit of power, "who changeth not." If the church has "begun in the Spirit," let us not attempt to change God's methods to complete our course in the weakness of human flesh. Since it is the Father's pleasure to "give good gifts to them who ask Him," it must be our pleasure to receive them humbly.[6]

In the days of Jesus and the first disciples, the power for signs, wonders, healings, miracles and deliverance was not just to authenticate the message; this power was *the expression of the message.* Signs and wonders were not just performed to validate the Good News; they were a vital element *of* the Good News! To put it another way, miracles do not primarily prove doctrine about God, so much as they reveal the nature of God. God has not changed. Neither has the Gospel message. God moves in power, in signs and wonders—healing the sick, in deliverances, multiplying food for the hungry, raising the dead—primarily for this reason: He is good! And it is His desire to reveal His *goodness*—His glory—in all the earth.

Ministries on the Move

One of the most exciting developments of this renewal move-ment and its ensuing wave of missions is seeing God invade the earth with a fresh and powerful revelation of His glory among the nations. God is making Himself seen, heard and felt in all the ways that many once only read about in the Bible. Jesus Christ, who is the same yesterday, today and forever, is reminding us that every page of God's Word is still valid and true for today because He Himself, the Living Word, has not changed.

Personally, I believe we are living in the grace of this out-pouring of power because we are moving toward the *last* days, the days of the final harvest. I believe a few ministries in particular embody what God is doing in these last days throughout the earth. I have already introduced you in chap-ter 4 to Rolland and Heidi Baker of Iris Ministries. Let me now introduce you to the founder of Global Missions Aware-ness, Leif Hetland, whose story I will relate. I also want to introduce you to Steve and Christina Stewart of Impact Na-tions, and Stacy and Casey Long of Catch the Fire USA, who will tell you their stories in their own words. Through their ministries, these believers share with everyone they touch both signs of love and wonders of compassion.

Leif Hetland, Norway/Alabama

A fourth-generation Christian growing up in Stavanger, Norway, Leif Hetland rebelled at the age of thirteen. Falling into a lifestyle of alcohol and drugs, he endured the ruth-less cold and hunger of the gutters for several years before returning home broken and confused to his family. Struggling with unresolved spiritual heart issues and unable to shake the grip of addiction, he led a double life until one night in January 1985. In the agony of detoxification, violently ill and raging with fever, Leif experienced the tangible presence of God in a powerful way. The sickness and fever instantly left, along with the addiction. More importantly, Leif experienced the "gift of forgiveness." Bitterness, hurt and anger melted from his heart. Forgiveness and acceptance were no longer just doctrine, but a heart revelation experienced through a sovereign touch of God. A central theme of Leif's ministry today is the truth that "God does not treat us according to our history, but according to our destiny."

In 1989 Leif married and earned a B.A. from Luther Rice University in Georgia. He took a position as youth pastor in a Presbyterian church, eventually returning to Norway to pastor a Baptist church. In the years that followed, Leif was a "closet charismatic." He stopped practicing what he believed because he did not want to run the risk of losing his reputation or his church. By 1994 he had become the classic burned-out high achiever living *for* God, not living *from* God.

In May 1994, one of Leif's elders invited him to travel to England to meet with some pastors who had been to Toronto. During the series of meetings, Leif received prayer, prophetic words were spoken over him and God began a deep healing process. Leif and his friend returned to Norway to find that an anointing had been imparted to them during their time in England. Renewal immediately broke out in their church, and many people experienced dramatic healings. Then while Leif was out of the country, one of the influential elders, disturbed by some of the abuses of the gifts, began to teach that this was not of God. As a result, the renewal in their church was quenched.

In 1995, I went to Norway to meet with a group of a hundred pastors at Haugesund Mission Church. When Leif came forward for prayer, I prophesied, "You are a bulldozer . . . going into areas that have been untouched. I see a multitude of people coming out of darkness and following you into the light."

Leif went out in the Spirit, weeping for two and a half to three hours. He knew a transference of anointing had taken place. Following that conference, Leif held two conferences of his own in which he noticed a large increase in healings and salvations—yet he had not done anything differently. Before, if someone got healed, it was like winning the lottery—great, but rare. Now, it was the *norm* to see people get healed physically and also emotionally through prophetic words.

"Before," Leif says, "I prayed for the sick but didn't really expect God to do much. My attitude was, *Oh well, God is sovereign.* Now there was a whole different expectancy as God's calling was released in my life. There was this 'week of glory' shortly after Randy's impartation where everyone I prayed for got healed, addicts were delivered upon a single touch and all the gifts of the Spirit were operating through me. It was actually scary! I thought I was losing my mind because I saw people through Jesus' eyes and could feel their pain when I touched them. This didn't continue, but I believe God was giving me a taste of what is supposed to be the normal Christian life when we are walking in the fullness of the Spirit."

Leif forgot about my prophecy for about a year and a half. During this time he seriously injured his neck in a pool accident and his back in a car wreck. He was in and out of the hospital for eighteen months. During this extended time in bed, the Holy Spirit reminded him of my words. He began to sense a tremendous, supernatural burden for the unreached in the world—there are over 70 million people in Arab nations who have never heard the name of Jesus! He knew he was supposed to go where no one else was going.

At the end of 1996 Leif's friend, Bjornar Heimstad, invited Leif to go to Pakistan. In confirmation of my prophetic word, that was the start of many trips to Pakistan, where Leif would see thousands upon thousands healed and saved. By the grace of God, he has now been in over 76 countries, many of them Muslim and some of them Communist.

"I know God is treating me according to His chosen destiny for me, certainly not according to my merit!" Leif says. "He has granted me unprecedented favor with national leaders, with religious leaders, even with heads of state. He is the One opening doors no man can shut! I have seen every kind of miracle you can imagine—tumors dropping off, creative miracles where missing parts are restored, blind eyes seeing, everything. God is revealing His glory! Through the revelation of His glory, His goodness and compassion, hundreds of thousands are coming to Christ in areas that are officially closed to the Gospel."

In 2000 Leif's ministry took a dramatic turn. By this time he had been forced to resign from the Baptist Church in the U.S., primarily due to his association with the Toronto Blessing. Wounded and hurting, Leif attended a Father-Son weekend where the ministry team included Jack Taylor, Charles Carrin and worship leader Dennis Jernigan. Dennis came to Leif and asked to pray for him. He ended up singing "The Father's

Song" over Leif while the Holy Spirit poured out what Leif calls "a baptism of love."

"My whole message changed that day," Leif says. "My Abba Father revealed Himself to me. I was healed of my 'orphan spirit' and received the 'spirit of sonship.' I learned that my inheritance is something I receive, not something I must achieve. My Father was giving me the nations not because of anything I did, but because I'm his son! I went home from that weekend a changed man. I went home a lover, not a doer. Ask my wife and kids!"

In the last eleven years, Leif has trained thousands of pastors, mostly in closed and hostile areas of the world. He gets letters every week from those to whom he has passed on the impartation he received from me. He explains, "The prayer of impartation is like being impregnated with what the Spirit is stirring and will bring to birth."

Leif's message is clear. The Great Commandment—to love—must come before the Great Commission—to do. "I've stepped back from the 'work' of ministry, and now I just play with my Daddy. The wonderful thing is that I'm seeing more fruit than ever! God is love. When His love is released, healing comes—healing of every kind."[7]

Leif's ministry has been an amazing conduit of God's glory. The signs, wonders and miracles worked through him and the Word proclaimed by him have brought a revelation of God's goodness to more than 986,000 in Pakistan, the Philippines, Cuba and many other nations around the world in recent years. Multiply that by how God is working through all Leif's spiritual "sons" (who are also my spiritual grandsons), and one can get a small grasp on how God is pouring out His Spirit in these last days.

But Leif is not the only one. Steve Stewart related the following amazing story of impartation and its fruits to me. He tells it here in his own words:

Steve Stewart
Vancouver, British Columbia

In 1994 I was pastoring the Cambridge Vineyard near Toronto. Five days into the outbreak of renewal, John Arnott called me to come over and witness what was happening at the Toronto Airport Christian Fellowship [then called Toronto Airport Vineyard]. As I stood at the back of the auditorium during worship, a bit dumbfounded at what was going on, I saw John beckoning for me to come down to see something at the front. Two of my four sons, ages nine and ten, were shaking on the floor! My twelve-year-old was prophesying over them! I had no frame of reference for this. The reaction going through my mind was, **We're good Presbyterian stock. We don't do this!**

John called all of us pastors into another room, where he and Randy prayed for us. Now, the Vineyard did not believe in the "falling down" stuff, but the power of God fell and down we went. After about two minutes I got up, looked at the pastors out cold around me and asked John, "What happened?" John had a sore throat, so I offered to pray for him—just a simple prayer. I reached out to touch his neck. Later, people described to me what happened next. When I touched John, they said it looked like two bowling pins colliding. We both spun out and flew several feet across the room in different directions.

I stayed in the spot where I landed from 9:00 p.m. until 1:00 a.m. In those hours, everything changed! As I lay on the floor, the power of God coursed through me in waves of electricity and light. I could not stand; I could not talk. Carol Arnott and someone, I do not know who, propped me up and began helping me lay hands on other people. As soon as I did, they would explode into various manifestations. This completely befuddled me!

The next day I had calmed down somewhat, and I met with the staff in my church office. No one could work. We just began to worship. Throughout the day, as others came into the office from the parking lot, they would simply fall to the floor and begin weeping.

That next night, back at Airport Vineyard, John called me up to share. I told about how I had been so dry for the past eight years. Randy laid hands on me again, and again, the power of God surged through me and I could not speak. For the next several months I was frequently overcome with stuttering, and I still sometimes stutter whenever the presence of God is manifesting.

The next Sunday in my church, I shared my testimony. This was a church where no one had ever fallen, but the whole church fell out in the 9:00 service. When the 11:00 people came, they had to step over the bodies. Then they started falling out, the presence of God was so heavy. People finally started getting up to leave around 3:30, but decided to come back in the evening—even though we had never had a Sunday evening service.

A few weeks later, I left for Russia and stopped to speak for one night at a conference in Stockholm. As I stood at the podium, I felt the Holy Spirit coming on and thought, "Oh no, Lord. Not here! I only have one night with these people, and I've got to preach what I have for them." I decided to stare at the ground and concentrate really hard on staying upright. Well, the translator next to me fell down! Another came up, and he fell down! And the next! I finally decided to quit fighting the Holy Spirit and announced, "I guess we're done." At that moment, the Holy Spirit fell on the whole place.

As I continued my trip, the same thing happened in Russia and Brazil—even though I had determined to say nothing about what was happening in Toronto. The Holy Spirit was showing up, and we were seeing a tremendous increase in physical healings as well.

In 1995, my wife, Christina, and I moved to Vancouver to start a new church. We have also started a ministry called Impact Nations. This grew out of our realization that what Randy had imparted to me that night was not just meant for a great one-time experience or even for a few nights. It has lasted all these years, and we have imparted to many thousands of others. We have traveled and ministered in healing to many nations, and we keep getting testimonies from those whom it has impacted. For a number of years we were doing a lot of seminars for businesspeople, and some of them are being used by God so powerfully that they tell me, "Steve, I don't know if I'm running a business or a ministry."

Doors continue to open for Impact Nations that we never expected. We now run three branches of ministry—seminars for training and equipping leaders, development projects and something we call Journeys of Compassion. Our development projects include medical clinics, feeding centers, farms, helping the poor start businesses, micro-credit and providing clean drinking water and sewing schools for women-at-risk. Here is a journal entry from just one day at a medical clinic:

We opened the gate and let the first hundred come in for medical treatment. Several team members moved among those waiting for treatment, offering to pray. Almost all of them immediately responded with an eager, "Yes, please." As the team prayed, something began to shift; we could all feel the heaviness around this place beginning to lift. Someone was healed, and then another, and another. There was a rising excitement—some people began to clap and shout as God's healing mercy and power moved like a wave through the crowd. Before the morning was over, four totally blind people were instantly and completely healed.[8]

The Journeys of Compassion involve sending out teams on short-term missions trips. Every team member ministers on the front lines, directly engaged in both supernatural and practical demonstrations of the Kingdom of God. In April 2006, such a missions team headed into the North-East province of Kenya, which was 90 percent Muslim. There, we held open-air healing and evangelism meetings in a large field in the middle of the capital city, Garissa. In the beginning, many Muslims came, but observed from a safe distance. As the meetings continued, more and more came forward. From the first meeting, God broke out with healing and miracles, reports of which spread all over the city. Here are a few healings that took place: A fifteen-year-old girl born deaf was completely healed. Another deaf and mute girl was healed and spoke her first word ever—Jesus! Several blind eyes were opened—including a young child who began to look around [in surprise]. Malaria fevers instantly left. Hundreds of people had long-standing pain leave. Hemorrhaging stopped. As the power of Christ was revealed among the Muslims and other Africans, many raised their hands to receive the Lord. Two of the team members shared the

Gospel with a group of about thirty children who had come early—they all prayed to ask Jesus into their lives. It was such a privilege to witness this historic breakthrough in the Muslim-dominated N.E. province.[9]

More recently, in May 2012, we saw some amazing demonstrations of God's power in Kenya's Nakuru prison. We did a baptism there on a Saturday, and on Monday six men were taken from the prison to court for sentencing. As is the custom before sentencing, the judge asked if the first man had anything to say. The young man replied, "I am now a born-again Christian who was baptized on Saturday in the prison. I am a new man."

The judge then asked if this young man was one of those baptized in the tank in the prison—he had seen it on national television. All six men told him that they had been baptized. The judge looked at them for some time, then did something that **never** happens. He gave them all a suspended sentence, conditional upon them staying out of trouble for six months.

It was unbelievable, but only the beginning. Next, the prison chaplain informed us that 152 **prison guards** had asked to be baptized at the next baptism. Amazing! Then the president of the biggest television network in Kenya called to say that the network decided to show the prison baptism on national television **four** times. They had never shown any news story that often since he was the president of the company.[10]

Outside the prison, in a very poor area of Nakuru, many people came to Christ through our team's ministry. Cataracts disappeared, long-standing pain left. Several of the team preached and prayed powerful prayers over the crowd. By the end of the journey, 1,380 people had not only come to Christ—they had given their contact information and are being integrated into local churches, including a weekly Bible study for 56 Muslims who came to Jesus. Each Journey of Compassion like this yields untold fruit for the Kingdom of God.

What was given to me through impartation has been multiplied many, many times over. We train people, and then we get out of the way and let them do the ministry. This philosophy goes all the way back to 1994 when Randy imparted to me. Impartation is reproducible. That is how the Kingdom of God multiplies![11]

Stacy and Casey Long
Catch the Fire USA National Coordinators

[The impartation Stacy and Casey Long received has set them on fire to spread revival across the United States and around the world. I want to let Stacy tell us about it in his own words.]

I admit it was not my most godly moment, but there I was on the back row of the church, genuinely pouting. Coming from a nondenominational church, I had never heard a message on impartation and the transfer of anointing. Randy Clark did such a good job of explaining it, using so many Scriptures, that I was absolutely convinced and thought, **This is for me.** So I almost rudely pushed my way to the front of the church during impartation time and assumed the "receiving" position, with my hands out. I put the most desperate look on my face that I could muster. After all, I wanted Randy to know that I was desperate. I cracked open one eye to see if he saw me. **He sees me; he's coming; he's coming. He's going to pray for me for a** long time, and I'm going to fall down, laugh, cry, shake and be changed forever. Or so I thought. That is what other people were doing.

I heard Randy praying for a woman next to me, then suddenly a thumb thrust into my right palm and I heard the words "Bless him, Lord." Then Randy walked away.

I opened my eyes in a little bit of shock and thought to myself, That was it? That's all I get? Nothing happened! I hung my head, made my way to the back row where my wife was sitting and began to sulk.

"What happened?" my wife asked.

"Nothing happened," I told her. "He said 'Bless him, Lord,' and then he walked away." I was truly disappointed. I knew I needed what Randy was talking about.

Just then my right palm, the exact place where Randy touched me, began to burn. Then my left palm began to burn. Then my legs and hands started shaking. I screamed out, "Something happened, something happened!" And something did happen! My life and the life of my family would never be the same after that.

My family and I had been preparing to move to Bosnia as missionaries, and this impartation took place two months before we left. The best miracle we had seen up to that point was when we prayed for someone's headache, and two days and many Advil later, it was gone. But we moved to Bosnia and began to see healings, dramatic deliverances, the prophetic flowing and people getting saved in supernatural ways.

One such supernatural salvation happened with a friend whom I will call Mark. His earliest memory was of his dad raping his older sister. His dad beat him, his sisters and his mom daily. When Mark was fourteen, the war was taking place and his diabetic mom could not get insulin. As a result, she had to have her leg amputated. While visiting her in the hospital, Mark heard his dad's drunken voice in the hallway. He looked out to see his dad give the doctors and nurses money. Mark watched them all walk away, and he knew something bad was about to happen. He hid behind a curtain as his dad proceeded to rape his mother and beat her newly amputated leg until she died.

We met Mark when he was around twenty years old. To say that he had some anger issues would be an understatement. He started coming to our worship and soaking meetings because of the love, acceptance and presence of God that he felt. One night in our soaking meeting, Mark was slowly pacing back and forth across the living room, praying or worshiping. I was doing the same when I noticed that Mark had stopped and was just standing in one place, staring down at the floor. I had the urge to go over and pray for him, but did not want to interrupt his personal time with God. After a while I went over, gently laid hands on his shoulders and prayed a short prayer: "Holy Spirit, You have to help him."

Just then he fell forward with his hands to his sides, as though he had fainted. Another friend and I caught him just before he smashed his face into the ground. He was instantly soaking wet with sweat, bright red and shaking intensely. He kept looking around fearfully, saying, "Where did you take me? How long have I been gone? Where did you take me?"

It took us over an hour to convince him that he has not taken him anywhere, that it was the same day and that we did not put drugs in his drink. He hardly believed us. Apparently, he had a three-day-long encounter that occurred in the half second between me praying, "Holy Spirit, help him" and our catching him before he face planted. He was in a field, and Jesus walked up to him and had what looked like a light shining out from behind His head. Mark saw a group of angels hovering in the air, singing sounds that we do not have here on earth. Mark said it was so beautiful that he wanted to just sit there forever and listen. Jesus took him to a sand dune desert and left him there. Mark began to run in fear for hours and hours, screaming our names until he collapsed. (That is apparently why he was bright red and dripping with sweat.)

While Mark was running in the desert, Jesus spoke to him from the sky about lies and truth. Jesus then took Mark to his mom's funeral. There he was as a twenty-year-old, standing with Jesus and watching himself as a fourteen-year-old at his mom's funeral. Everything was exactly the way he remembered it, except for one detail that was highlighted. When everyone was almost done piling dirt back onto his mother's casket, he saw his uncle throw two Catholic trinkets into the dirt. He had not seen that happen in real life.

Jesus took Mark back and showed him every hurtful thing that his dad ever did to him. He became increasingly enraged at the damage and pain that his dad had caused. Then Jesus began to show him every moment and incident where Mark had caused someone else pain. His heart began to soften as he realized that he was guilty, just like his dad. Then the encounter ended.

As Mark described this encounter, I was completely flabbergasted at the awesomeness of God. Mark, on the other hand, was not convinced that it was from God. He kept trying to say it was because of stress and that he was not sleeping enough and had not been eating the proper foods.

He figured that was why this crazy thing had happened to him. No matter how hard I tried, I could not convince him that this encounter was from God.

"There's only one way to find out if this is true or not," Mark told me.

"How?" I asked.

He said, "I have to go to my mother's grave." He begged and pleaded for me to go with him to his mother's grave and help him dig in the middle of the night, but I refused. Mark's apartment building backed up to the enormous city cemetery where his mother was buried. He left my house that night around 1:00 a.m., went home, grabbed a flashlight and a spade, hopped the graveyard fence and approached his mother's grave. He bent down and started to dig right around the spot where he had seen his uncle throw the trinkets in the grave during the "encounter." As he dug down several inches, it hit him. **I'm desecrating my mother's grave in the middle of the night!** he thought. **What am I doing?** Just then his spade caught something metal.

Around 11:00 the next morning, I got a knock on my door. I opened it to see Mark. "I found them!" he said.

Goose bumps went up and down my entire body, and the wind was almost knocked out of my chest. He told me the story of what had happened at the grave. As he dug up those metal trinkets, a wave of realization hit him—the encounter was all true. Already on his knees, he began to weep uncontrollably and cry out, "Jesus! I believe You. It's true! I need You! Help me! My life is Yours!"

Mark gave his life to Jesus on his mother's grave in the middle of the night, and he has never been the same since. This is just one of the amazing stories of God's incredible grace that we have been a part of, and just one of hundreds of testimonies of the power of impartation to affect lives.[12]

Just Because

This chapter started with two questions: "Why impartations? Why signs and wonders?" Do they occur to validate a message? I believe that this is sometimes the case, but more importantly, I believe God does good things just because He is good. He works acts of love just because He is love. Signs and wonders, miracles and healings are just God *being* God and revealing His glory to a world that is desperately ignorant of His true nature. Does He need any other reason?

God reveals His glory through His signs of love and wonders of compassion. Without His impartation of power and love, we would be unable to do His signs of love and wonders of compassion. And in our inability to reflect our heavenly Father, we would take away from the glory that we should be bringing Him by bearing much fruit.

But that is not the case. He does good things because He is good, and He gives us the ability to reflect His glory through much wondrous fruit. And so His Word in Habakkuk 2:14 is being fulfilled, "For the earth will be filled with the knowledge of the glory of the Lord, as the waters cover the sea."

7

Radical Obedience

Impartation for the Power to Die

When I preach on the subject of impartation and know that I am going to pray for people afterward, I always share Heidi Baker's experience and the wonderful fruit that has occurred since she received an impartation. Often, after asking the people, "How many of you would like to receive an impartation like Heidi Baker received?" almost everyone raises their hands. I then say, "Now, let me tell you the rest of the story." Then I tell them about all the suffering and hardships the Bakers faced within eighteen months of Heidi's experience of impartation. I point out that often there is a degree of difficulty corresponding to the degree of the intensity of the impartation. I do not understand how it all works; all I am sure of is that the price of revival is high and that impartations prepare people to be willing to pay that price.

While praying for people to receive an impartation, I do not just ask God to fill them with power; I also ask that He baptize them in His love. I know that it is the baptism of love that will keep them from quitting when the going gets tough. It is the baptism of power that gives them the ability to minister, but it is the baptism of love that gives them the motivation to minister, and to keep on ministering, especially in missions.

My friend Graham Cooke told me about a training event he and Jonathan David, an apostolic leader from Indonesia, conducted in the Philippines. They were training about seventy young leaders who were going into China and other places where the preaching of the Gospel could result in prison and/or death (this was in the mid- to late-1990s). One young woman came to the two leaders and told them about having a vision of her death as a martyr. Later a second person had a similar vision, this time a young man. Then another young man came with tears in his eyes, deeply burdened in his soul. He asked the question, "Is there something displeasing in my life that the Lord would not consider me worthy of being martyred for His sake?" This is the fruit of those who have had a powerful impartation from the Holy Spirit.

The apostolic leader Sophal Ung of Cambodia experienced deep suffering under both the Khmer Rouge and the Vietnamese. He was one of the first young Cambodians to be led to the Lord in the 1970s. He was powerfully filled with the Holy Spirit during an experience where the Holy Spirit blew open the window of an upper room where the believers were praying and filled them. They began to either speak in tongues or prophesy. Later, almost 90 percent of his congregation would be killed in the Killing Fields or in other places by the Khmer Rouge soldiers. After being tortured himself, put in a prison dungeon and being the sole survivor out of about two hundred prisoners, he miraculously escaped and eventually made his way to the United States with his wife and five children. Not long after coming to the States, his wife died of cancer. God then called Sophal Ung back to Cambodia. This was the hardest thing he had ever heard from God. He would have to leave his five children in America to be cared for by other friends and family. Sophal Ung's life is a life of miracles, a life of sacrifice and faith.

Only a baptism of love and power could give someone the ability to face the prospect of torture and death, to leave behind five biological and two adopted children and the safety and comfort of the United States and to return to the war-stricken and impoverished country of Cambodia. I personally interviewed Sophal Ung on our first trip to Cambodia in 2003. We went back in 2010 and interviewed him again, and from several hours of interviews we are putting together a powerful book about his life and ministry. I believe he is the greatest apostle in the nation of Cambodia, and his heart burns for the salvation of his nation. When he visited Toronto Airport Christian Fellowship, he experienced such a powerful new filling of the Holy Spirit that it affected his body until he shook and trembled under the power. He said his body movements were similar to what happened when the Vietnamese tortured him with electrical prods—but instead of bringing weakness and pain, the power of God brought joy, strength and boldness. He then encouraged any Cambodians in the United States who were considering returning to their country to help in the ministry to first go with him to Toronto and receive from God.

The Family Sacrifice

My friend Guy Chevreau and I were talking one night about the cost of living our lives for Christ and working in this renewal/revival. We agreed that we felt everything we had paid was worth it. We agreed that nothing really should be counted as a sacrifice in light of how God has reached down and touched us, empowered us and sent us to the nations. Then Guy said to me, "That is, nothing is a sacrifice except the cost to our families. Every time the offering plate comes by, I put my hand in it and purpose in my heart that my family is placed in the offering."

I agreed. While we have not left our children behind in the way that Sophal Ung had to do, we were both spending about 180 days a year away from our wives and children. Once, when flying with Rolland and Heidi Baker in Mozambique, we began to talk about what a privilege it was to see a revival, a people movement, a harvest of souls accompanied by miracles of healings, deliverances and provision. Yet we all agreed that our families had paid a very high price. We knew that at least half of our children's lives were spent separated from us. We encouraged ourselves that God would be faithful to touch our children and somehow redeem the time we had to spend away from them.

In comparison to other periods of missionary expansion, however, we are living in a better time. In the nineteenth-century modern missionary movement, missionaries often had to leave their children in the care of grandparents or aunts and uncles because they realized there was a high mortality rate for children in the country where they would be serving. Other missionaries like the Baptists' Hudson Taylor and

Adoniram Judson, two great pioneer missionaries to China and to Burma, buried wives and children in the soil of their mission fields. Rolland's own grandparents buried two children in the remote mountains of Tibet.

I believe we are living in a better time, but we cannot ignore that there is still a price to pay. It is easy to say, "Yes, I want the anointing! I want an impartation!" It is another thing to be willing to pay the price. People see the wonderful, amazing revival going on in Mozambique and the surrounding nations today through Iris Ministries. What they rarely see are the ever-present struggles, battles and sacrifices the Bakers face. When Rolland's dear friend Mel Tari heard about the writing of this book, he urged my editor (who was Rolland's sister, Linda Kaahanui), "Please, whatever you do, don't leave people with the impression that the anointing is something you can just run down to the altar for, and *bang*, through one quick experience, you have a powerful ministry."

Mel is right. God worked for seventeen years in the hearts of Rolland and Heidi, bringing them to a place where they were humble and obedient servants willing to be completely poured out. Revival is not just about power—or even primarily about power. More importantly, it is about love and humility. Are we willing to allow the Holy Spirit to do whatever it takes to break us of our pride, our need to control, our self-seeking motives in ministry? Are we desperate enough for God to let Him completely have His way in us?

In April 1999 I was in Redding, California, to minister with my friend Bill Johnson at Bethel Church. Somehow Heidi and I ended up at Bill's church at the same time. I had heard that wonderful things were happening with Heidi and that she had been powerfully touched through the prophecy

I gave her in January 1997. Up until this time, I had not been able to meet Heidi personally, nor had I really understood the magnitude of what God had been doing through her and Rolland. I also did not realize the high cost their family had paid as a result of "walking out" the prophetic word. In two years there had been over 250 churches planted! But this was not accomplished with a great missionary force and an entire denomination behind them. This was a truly miraculous increase from just one church, twelve Mozambican leaders and Rolland and Heidi.

At Bethel Church, I heard Heidi's testimony for the first time as she preached a powerful sermon on walking by faith. For the first time, I understood how significant that prophetic word had been and how much suffering the Bakers had been through in obedience to walking out the promises of that word.

It is not enough to simply have someone pray for you or prophesy over you. That word from the Lord must be met with faith, taken hold of and walked in. God had a destiny for the children of Israel when He led them out of Egypt. Yet unbelief kept that generation from ever reaching the land of God's promise. Rolland, Heidi, Leif and others like them are walking in God's promised destiny for their lives, but not simply because of a single act of impartation or prophecy. It is because they have chosen to receive by faith what God has promised, whatever the cost, and have determined to lay everything else down in reckless love for Jesus, in total submission to His every leading.

Heidi once told me how she picks her leadership in Mozambique. One of the things she does is to bring pastors to the orphanage to see how they minister to, play with and love on the children. If they do not have true love for the children and a willingness to serve them, then she feels they do not have enough of a servant's heart to be considered a key leader. She looks for love and service.

I found one of the most powerful illustrations of this type of love and servant's heart in an email from Rolland referring to a dangerous cholera epidemic that had broken out some time ago at their ministry center in Zimpeto. Many children were fighting for their lives, and the medical profession believed many would die from the cholera. They thought the disease was introduced by contaminated food brought to a wedding in their church. Wildly contagious, within days cholera had decimated seventy children, pastors and workers, who had to be taken to a special cholera hospital in Maputo. This was actually a big, strictly quarantined tent full of "cholera tables," bare wooden beds with a hole in each one and buckets underneath for the nonstop diarrhea and vomiting. Every patient was on an IV drip. Rolland told the story best in an Iris Ministries newsletter following the outbreak:

> Maputo's health officials were terrified of a citywide epidemic. Maputo's Director of Health put her finger in Heidi's face and told her, "You will be responsible for killing half of Maputo!" . . . Soon the city police were involved, intent on shutting down our entire center and ministry. For days nothing seemed to help. We were washing and disinfecting everything. Our trucks were making hospital runs day and night. Our own clinic was filled with children on IVs. Our staff was completely exhausted.
>
> Only Heidi was allowed to visit the tent hospital. Every day she would go in and spend hours and hours with our kids, holding them, soaking them in prayer, declaring that they would live and not die. They vomited on her, covered her

131

with filth, and slowly grew weaker. Many were on the edge of
death, their eyes sunken and rolling back. The doctors were
shocked by her lack of concern for herself, and were certain
she would die along with many of our children.[1]

All during this time, the Holy Spirit kept falling on the
Bakers' meetings. Rolland relates that a strong spirit of intercession came over their stronger pastors, who would pray
all hours for the cholera victims and the suffering of the
whole nation. Intercessory prayer groups in the U.S., Canada
and around the world joined them. The entire future of the
ministry in Mozambique was in question and the staff was
exhausted, and then some of the children began coming home
from the hospital and there were no more new cases! "Extraordinary" was the only word they could use to describe it.
Just like that, the cholera was gone, and through it all Heidi
was fine. In the newsletter, Rolland related the stunned reaction of the medical personnel outside their ministry:

> The doctors and nurses at the hospital are in a state of shock
> and wonder. The Director of Health again put a finger in
> Heidi's face: "You! This is God! The only reason you got
> through this was God! You and dozens of these children
> should be dead!"
>
> Eight of the medical staff there want to work with us now.
> "This is miraculous! You know God! We've never seen God
> do anything like this. We've never seen such love! We don't
> want to work here anymore. We want to work with you!"
> And so they will.

The Bakers did not lose a single person who lived with them
at Zimpeto at the time of the outbreak. In a matter of days,
the worst crisis they ever faced turned into waves of peace

and joy at the center, and their response was to worship the Lord at all hours, beholding His beauty in their hearts and enjoying His company.

At one of our past conferences, Rolland and Heidi shared how high the attrition rate is for North Americans who go on the field as long-term missionaries. Unless they have an experience of empowerment from the Holy Spirit, many do not last very long. A great price must be paid for the pursuit of God and for the desire to be a disciple who not only tries to obey God's ethical commands, but to obey His command to heal the sick, cast out demons, preach the Good News to the poor and raise the dead.

In another email Rolland sent me, he talked about his first trip into the Congo, which he took with Surprise Sithole. In the midst of describing the hardships of the people and the trip, Rolland stated,

> This movement does not chase health and wealth, or manifestations, or signs and wonders. We preach Jesus and Him crucified, and the power of the Cross. Nothing counts but faith working through love, producing joy! We seek first His Kingdom and His righteousness, and all these other things will chase us! We are learning how to be rich in good deeds, and blessed with godliness and contentment. We are falling in love with Him who is love, until nothing in this world attracts us like He does. . . .
>
> After all these years of preaching in the bush among the poor and faraway, we realize we have seen just the beginning of what God plans for Africa. North Africa, considered almost off-limits for the Christian Gospel, is beckoning. Jesus has no competition once His reality, love and power are known. Angola and West Africa are calling. The multitudes want what is real. Our bodies are exhausted, our time is stretched

beyond endurance, our wisdom for shepherding this movement is finite, but each morning we find ourselves renewed by the power of God. These pastors in Bukavu are ready to preach all across the Congo, taking the fire of God everywhere they go. We must encourage them; we must do our part; we must obey. Our lives are worth nothing to us, if only we may finish the race and complete the task the Lord Jesus has given us—the task of testifying to the gospel of God's grace (Acts 20:24).[2]

What is revival all about? Sacrifice being made? Yes. Joy being present? Yes. Love reaching out to others? Yes. Intimacy with God in the secret place? Yes. I can hear the pleas of Heidi as I write, "Lower still, lower still, lower still, the river flows to the lowest place, lower still, lower still." She is ever crying out for a greater willingness to lay down her life, her pride and her own desires.

The Nets Are Breaking!

What are the twin engines that have driven this move of God, this new missionary movement around the world? They are *intimacy with God* and *humility before God*. These two engines have been fueled by love and power, impartations and gifts. I used impartations in the plural on purpose, for I know of several impartations Heidi has received and one that Rolland has received since the initial prophecy I gave her in Toronto. It is not a one-time experience, but one that will need to be repeated as we pour ourselves out on His behalf to those in need. We who are willing to "spend and be spent" (2 Corinthians 12:15, RSV) for the salvation of souls need to occasionally have our own lives renewed by a fresh impartation of the Holy Spirit.

Do you want to be part of this new missionary movement? I have given you the key to being used by God: intimacy and humility, and faith and the hunger to ask God for a powerful impartation of the Holy Spirit. Some of you may never have had the experience of being filled with or baptized in the Holy Spirit. Others may have had this experience, but you need a fresh new filling, or you need an impartation for certain gifts to increase your fruitfulness in His Kingdom. Perhaps you need the gifts of healings, the gift of faith for miracles, the gift of word of knowledge or whatever God has for you.

Actually, these gifts often come in tandem. For example, the gifts of healings are often connected to the gift of word of knowledge; the gift of working of miracles is connected to the gift of faith; the gift of prophecy to the gift of discernment; and the gift of tongues to the gift of interpretation of tongues. So I encourage you to ask and keep on asking, knock and keep on knocking, seek and keep on seeking. I remind you of the words of the apostle Paul: "But eagerly desire the greater gifts," and "Follow the way of love and eagerly desire spiritual gifts, especially the gift of prophecy" (1 Corinthians 12:31; 14:1).

During the writing of this book's revised edition, Rolland Baker flew to meet me in Washington State so that we could go over the details that had to do with Iris Ministries in this manuscript. When we came to the section on Mozambique, he told me, "Help is desperately needed. The nets are breaking! Unless more help comes to the Mozambican people, many converts will be lost. The few workers are becoming exhausted. Hands are becoming limp from the burden of the weight of the harvest."

What is happening in Mozambique today can be defined as a "people movement." You can read the full story of what God is doing there in the Bakers' book *Always Enough: God's Miraculous Provision among the Poorest Children on Earth* (Chosen, 2003). A people movement occurs when the Holy Spirit is working in a very special way, and everyone in a certain area is ready to accept Jesus. I made a commitment to myself that if I was ever privileged to witness a true people movement, I would do all I could to try to get workers to the harvest field to reap the harvest before it was lost. So I encourage you to consider going with me or one of my associates to Mozambique. You can come join us in the nations! Perhaps you will find new meaning for your life as you lay it down for Him. Several people who have traveled with me are now going to Mozambique regularly as short-term missionaries, and several churches have become partners with the Bakers as a result of seeing firsthand what God is doing through them. Pray to the Father that He would send forth laborers into His harvest. You could be among them, and literally millions of souls are at stake!

Be Clothed with Power

But first, before you go anywhere, I counsel you with the words of Jesus. "Stay in the [your] city until you have been clothed with power from on high"—this after he promised them, "I am going to send you what my Father has promised" (Luke 24:49). This was the promise of the Holy Spirit. I believe the reference here is not to the Spirit's work of regeneration, or to sealing the believer, but to the ministry of the Holy Spirit to "come upon" them and fill them with power from on high.

If you are a Christian, you have already been baptized by the Spirit into the Body of Christ (see Romans 8:9; 1 Corinthians 12:13). But I am counseling you beyond that to desire the mighty promise of the Father for the Spirit to come upon you and fill you with power for service. The next chapter contains some stories about what can happen when "little ole me" people are clothed with power. The willingness to die to self—and sometimes even to die as a martyr—is a fruit of such impartation and brings much fruit for the Kingdom, to the glory of God.

> I tell you the truth, unless a kernel of wheat falls to the ground and dies, it remains only a single seed. But if it dies, it produces many seeds. The man who loves his life will lose it, while the man who hates his life in this world will keep it for eternal life.
>
> John 12: 24–25

> But whatever was to my profit I now consider loss for the sake of Christ. What is more, I consider everything a loss compared to the surpassing greatness of knowing Christ Jesus my Lord, for whose sake I have lost all things.
>
> Philippians 3:7–8

Let's pray together for the power and love—the radical obedience—to count all things as loss for the sake of knowing Christ and serving His Kingdom.

O Holy Spirit, work in our hearts today to produce a love that is extravagant for God. Give us a love so extravagant that we are willing to "waste" our lives on Him, poured out as costly perfume. Only You can produce this kind of sacrificial love for Jesus and the Father. We confess that we cannot crucify our flesh; this must be Your work. So come, come, Holy Spirit, and create in us the life of Christ.

8

Clothed with Power

Nobody Is Safe!

Before January 1994, I had heard several times through different speakers at various conferences,

A revival is coming. It will be a nameless, faceless revival where there will be no "God's man of power for the hour" superstars, but rather the emphasis will be upon the equipped saints of the Church. So many will be touched that, at large events where many healings and miracles were happening, reporters won't be able to find out who prayed for someone who just received a major miraculous healing. Why not? Because the saints have been equipped and the old distinction between clergy and laity has been replaced from understanding it to be the role of the clergy to pray for the sick, to understanding that the role of the clergy and all five-fold offices is to "equip the saints for the work of the ministry."[1]

I believe the outpourings in Toronto, later in Pensacola, Florida, and in Smithton, Missouri, were a fulfillment of this prophetic word, along with the outpourings at several evangelical colleges and also earlier through Rodney Howard-Browne.

For many years now, I have observed the practice of impartation and studied the Scriptures on this vital grace. God sovereignly chooses to anoint someone with the grace to lay hands on others. The person prayed for receives an impartation of power for healings, miracles and/or deliverances. Some receive an impartation through corporate or individual prayer, without the laying on of hands. Regardless of the method, people who receive an impartation are then mightily used to advance the Kingdom of God.

I noticed that during the early days of Pentecostalism, many of the men and women who went out and pioneered churches around the world were first touched by a powerful impartation of the Holy Spirit. Many received their unusual power through going to Azusa Street and either "praying through" in the upper room for the baptism in the Holy Spirit, or by having someone lay hands on them for this experience. Regardless of which of the two biblical ways of bestowing power occurred, the issue is that they did receive power. And as they went around the world with this restoration message, many others were built up in faith through their words. The Pentecostal message was the answer to half a century of expectant prayer that went up from the Church around the world. That prayer was based on the belief that God was about to restore to the Church the gifts and power of the first-century apostolic Church. This message created a desire for the impartation of new power, or an impartation for gifts of healing and miracles.[2]

Nearly forty years after the Azusa Street Revival, the Church experienced another visitation of the Holy Spirit. This one, from 1946 through 1949, was called the Latter Rain Revival. Once again hearts were set on fire, and once again revival would go quickly around the world. There was a strong emphasis again on healing and especially on impartation and prophecy. This movement, like the earlier Pentecostal movement, was the catalyst for a new round of missionary outreach around the world.[3]

About forty years after that, from 1992 through 1996, another movement began. This ongoing movement is again emphasizing and restoring to the Church the ability to receive renewing power for ministry. Once again, people are coming from around the world to receive an impartation and take it back to their countries. This movement, with its various streams that contribute to "the River" of outpouring, is producing a new missionary expansion in the world, and again thousands of new churches are being started.

This kind of empowered ministry is most needed if we are to see a revival of Christianity in Western Europe. Western Europe has lots of preachers and pastors working in its respective countries, but it contains a very small percentage of practicing Christians. Statistics for most of its nations indicate that only between 3 percent and 6 percent of the individuals attend church regularly. Western Europe needs another Patrick from Ireland to raise up a missionary movement characterized not only by the preaching of the Gospel, but also by faithful obedience to the Lord's command, "Heal the sick, raise the dead, cleanse the lepers, cast out demons" (Matthew 10:8, NASB).

The largest churches in most European countries are churches that do believe in the continuation of Jesus' ministry.

Many of these churches were started at the beginning of the last century, following the outbreak of the Pentecostal movement that restored the message of the Kingdom with power to the Church. Many of the other large churches in both Eastern and Western Europe have been started in the last few decades by Africans who believe in the continuation of the ministry of healing.

Pastor Henry Madava from Zimbabwe pastors one of the largest churches in Ukraine. He started by ministering in the schools in Zimbabwe, then he left his country to study aeronautical engineering for six and a half years. He did not attend seminary for training as a pastor, yet in 1990 the Lord asked him to start a church. Reluctant at first, he obeyed in 1992, after the Lord told him that he had a choice—to obey or to go back to his own country and follow his own plans, knowing that they would not be as successful as the plans the Lord had for him.

Pastor Madava discovered that his educational training gave him many skills that helped him in his ministry, but the power came in his impartation for deliverance and healing. His church in Kiev started with 200 people, and he jokes that it grew to 30—negative growth. He prayed for insight, and the Lord told him that he already had a miracle in his house. He asked himself *What do I have?* and realized that he needed to return to the ministry of casting out demons and healing the sick. Victory Christian Church then became known all over the city as the place where people could find deliverance and healing, and his ministry grew to 6,000 at the main church and another 20,000 to 25,000 in 290 churches they started across the country. Each of those churches continues to start other churches, and they also run 30 rehabilitation centers that help people break free of their addictions. I interviewed Pastor Madava not long ago, and he has now led over a million people to the Lord.[4]

Missions Advance with Revival

Advancement in missions has always followed periods of revival. This was true of the First and Second Great Awakenings, the 1858 Prayer Revival, the Welsh Revival, the Pentecostal Revival, the Latter Rain Revival, and it is true of the current outpouring of the Spirit that began in the 1990s. A fresh impetus for missions is characteristic of true revival because true revival renews people's first love. Then they love what God loves, which motivates them to go to the nations.

When I think of the key leaders who participated in the meetings in Toronto and what has happened since then, I see this evidential characteristic of true revival. Rolland and Heidi Baker are on fire for the nations of Africa. I think of Leif Hetland, who has ministered in over seventy countries since his impartation. I think of Wesley Campbell, who burns with his concern for children at risk among the nations. He both raises money to help them and is used of God to call others to minister to them. I think of the apostolic leader Ché Ahn, who was so powerfully touched in Toronto and who has been used to start an apostolic network of churches with a very strong commitment to planting churches around the world, particularly in Asia. I think of the hundreds of "little ole me's" who have taken vacation time and spent their savings to go on short-term missions trips around the world.

Just in the last nine years, we have seen about five thousand people go with our ministry, Global Awakening, to the nations.[5] While preaching in Toronto the last few times, I asked the question, "How many of you have been to a nation since you were touched in Toronto?" I was shocked to see how many had gone. It looked as though at least half had gone to another nation. I know that is not normal for the average congregation.

Global Awakening has been sending 12–19 teams a year to the nations, with 20–120 people on each team. As I write this from an airport lounge, I am on my way to São Paulo to join 299 young people for our annual Youth Power Invasion. These young people, all between 13 and 29 years old, will be the teachers, preachers and ministry team. Two weeks ago we sent out two of our interns to join Rolland and Heidi Baker for long-term work in Mozambique. Two more of our interns are leaving in five months to join Leif Hetland and help him in his missionary work.

In the spring of 2004, I was in Mozambique with a team. During that trip I received three independent, prophetic words within 24 hours that were all in agreement. The words came from Heidi Baker, Lesley-Ann Leighton (Heidi's "spiritual twin," who has a similar spirit and anointing) and prophetess Jill Austin. The word was, "Randy, God wants to know if you are willing to be the father of a new missionary movement."

Each time I said, "Yes!" But I felt several things about this word. First, I felt unqualified to lead a new missionary movement. I felt as though God must be calling several other leaders in the Church to also become fathers in this new missionary movement. And I sensed a total awareness of my inability to know what to do to accomplish this word. Now, years later, I have the peace of knowing what I learned from my friend Leif Hetland: "This is a promise, not a problem, and if it is a promise it must be received; if it is a problem it must be achieved."

I realized this word was way beyond my ability to achieve, so I had to rest and watch as God began to give it to me as a promise. With all God has done since then, I have been able to compile a new book about missions called *Supernatural Missions: The Impact of the Supernatural on World Missions* (Global Awakening, 2012). I also wrote a small book called *God Can Use Little Ole Me* (Destiny Image, 1998). Its title sums up my testimony and my basic message to the Church. I look at my past, my limitations and things that I considered failures, and I have a whole new appreciation for what Paul wrote in Ephesians 3:20–21 (emphasis added): "Now to him who is able to do immeasurably more than all we ask or imagine, according to *his power that is at work within us*, to him be glory in the church and in Christ Jesus throughout all generations, for ever and ever!"

God is to be glorified in and through His Church! He is glorified when we finally believe that it is not about what *we* can do, but all about what *He* will do through us by His power, if we will let Him. Let me share a few testimonies from people who thought of themselves as just a "little ole me" until they received a powerful touch from the Holy Spirit. I will relate the first story, then let the others tell you their stories in their own words. In each case, these people realized that God had a lot more for them than anything they had ever thought to "ask or imagine."

John Gordon, Illinois

John Gordon was a layman who had attended our church for a long time and was even on the board for several years.

John had never had a true experience with Christ; he would tell you in his own words that he had a false conversion. John became upset with me over all the healing stuff that was going on and being taught in our church. In John's mind, it was not of God. In spite of his unbelief, however, John would experience two powerful impartations that would forever change his life.

God gave John his first impartation in March 1984, during our church's healing conference with Blaine Cook. John was standing in the back of the packed-out church. His hand was against the wall. Blaine gave the invitation and said, "I don't want you to come to the front for prayer just because you want to. I want to see what God does, and whom he touches. Some of you will receive a gift of healing tonight. If you begin to cry or tremble; if you begin to feel heavy, like it is hard to stand up straight because of the glory of God; if your hands get hot or tingly; if you feel electricity upon your head or heat in your chest, then I want you to come to the front for prayer."

When John heard these words, he immediately said in unbelief, "That's a bunch of bull!" He no sooner got the words out of his mouth than the Spirit of God fell upon him. His hand that was against the wall began to feel like it was waking up after going to sleep. Then the other hand had the same feeling. Both hands began to shake, and the intensity increased dramatically—to the point that his hands became a blur. He felt the heat of God, he was bent over by the weight of God's glory and he was crying—not just tears, but loud cries. As he moved forward down the center aisle, he saw me and cried out, "Help me, Randy! Help me, Randy! Help me, Randy!" I asked what was wrong, to which he replied, "I have cried so hard my eye is killing me. I need to get my contact out, but I can't with my hands shaking like this."

I replied, "John, that could be a word of knowledge." (The preceding session had been about words of knowledge.) He scoffed, "You and those words of knowledge. I don't even believe in them." Then a fourteen-year-old girl, Tammy, said, "That is my eye. I just came from the eye doctor. I was told I have to have surgery on my eye."

John, who a minute earlier had mocked the words of the preacher, stopped shaking, turned and prayed for Tammy's eye. It was healed. It took only one minute in the anointing to turn a mocker of this kind of ministry into ministering himself in the very things he mocked.

Later in the service, John was standing by the pulpit. I was next to him and heard him say, "Oh, God, I can't stand anymore. You're going to kill me!" I had read biographical books about revivalists in the nineteenth century, thinking to myself that I had been born in the wrong century. I had read about Finney and Moody, both of whom made similar statements about believing they would die if God's power continued to flow into them. I had wanted to live in a time of revival. I knew John had not read such books. When I heard him say, "You're going to kill me," I said to myself, *I'm in revival.* John has never been the same, still seeing people healed in Illinois, perhaps more than most pastors in the region.

John had another powerful experience of the Holy Spirit that involved impartation for deliverance. John and I had been asked to pray for a woman who was having grand mal seizures. There had been demonic activity in her family, and it was believed that the seizures were demonic in nature. The night prior to praying for her, John had been attacked by an evil spirit while asleep. Crying out the name "Jesus," John was taken into an open vision where he saw this demonized woman being raped when she was sixteen years old. In the open vision, John was given specific information about the woman, along with the names of the two demons that had entered her as a result of this traumatic experience. As John and I prayed for the woman, the demons began to manifest. John went to her and spoke to the demons, calling them by name, which caused the woman to exhibit much stronger demonic manifestations. Then John commanded the two demons by name to come out of her, which they did.

John is still living out the fruit of that impartation to this day. Some time after it, he was driving by the Bethesda Cancer Institute in southern Illinois. As he passed it he said, "I'd like the opportunity to pray for one hundred cancer patients." A brief time later, John received a call from the director of the institute, who asked him to participate in a study to determine the effects of prayer upon patients. He wanted John to pray for one hundred patients! John agreed.

Several healings took place as a result of John's prayers, including one man who had a vision of John entering his hospital room to pray for him. This man was healed, and his faith exploded as a result. John's impartation took place decades ago, and he is still one of the most on-fire people I know in praying for healing and deliverance.

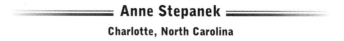

Anne Stepanek
Charlotte, North Carolina

I attended the first [Global Awakening] Healing School in Everett, Washington, in May 2004 with a friend. I'd been praying for the sick for about nine years with very minimal results, and I had never seen anyone instantly healed while I prayed for them. Well, the Healing School changed all that![6] On the last day of the school, I prayed for a woman with knee and back injuries, and she was instantly healed! The day we arrived back home in North Carolina, my friend prayed for a woman over the phone who was suffering with knee pain, and she was instantly healed! We continued to pray for the sick and saw more and more healings.

We were so excited that we trained up people in our church using Global Awakening's **Ministry Team Training Manual**. During the practice sessions of the training, people started getting healed! A six-year-old boy was prayed for at two practice sessions for a hole in his heart. The next week at his doctor's appointment, the hole was totally gone!

We saw an increase in healings in our church services, and also people began to pray for the sick in their workplaces and in stores, parks and doctors' offices. God miraculously healed many, some instantly and many within just a few days. It's just amazing what God is doing. I can't believe that God can use a little ole home school mom to release His healing power into the people I encounter as I just go about my day!

Carole Baerg
Toronto, Canada

It was January 1994 when my friends literally dragged me into a meeting at the Toronto Airport Vineyard. These dear friends had prepared a room in their house so I could stay with them during the last few weeks of my life. The doctors said there would only be six to twelve of them! I had been in so much pain for the past twenty years that I was looking forward to the end. Every day was a struggle to live.

When the ministry time came at the end of the service, my friends led me to Randy for prayer. When he laid his hands on me, I heard him say, "There is enough sadness in the Church, and you have been sad long enough!"

When Randy said that, I hit the deck, instantly "drunk" with joy! I don't remember much about the next two weeks, except that I was totally intoxicated with the love and joy of the Lord. One night, sitting up front, I just couldn't close my mouth. Randy came by and "poured more" into my mouth. This was only a symbolic gesture, but I realized the word spoken was "Open your mouth and He will fill it" (see Psalm 81:10). I was so drunk on the Holy Spirit that it took me three days to realize all my pain was gone!

After two weeks, I was asked to share my story at a women's conference. I was amazed to discover that as I tried to share, I could not speak because I was so overtaken with the Holy Spirit. I was helped to my seat! Later, many ladies came and asked if there was any way they could have what I had. What a shock to discover that I could "pass it on" to others!

Friends in ministry asked me to share, so I began to travel with them a bit. The Holy Spirit touched so many— healings, refreshing and lots of fun in the Holy Spirit. A team of pastors came from Europe in October 1994, and we prayed over them. When the top leader got off the floor, he asked if we would come to Belgium and share at the opening of his ministry center there. That's how I started going to Europe. From there it has been by word of mouth. When I first started to travel, it was such a surprise because I thought, **Women don't do this!**

The next year, when I was in Belgium, a woman came to me with her daughter who was eight to nine months pregnant. The baby was dead. Doctors had told her to wait another week for labor to deliver the dead fetus. I panicked! **I can't do this!** I thought. I began to pray, "Father, I have no faith for this . . ."

I couldn't tell if anything happened that day, but three years later, when I was in Belgium again, a young boy ran to me and threw his arms around me. He cried out, "I'm the miracle baby!" I met the grandmother and, sure enough, that boy was the one whom I had prayed for!

I am still discovering the gift that Randy imparted to me. In September 2004, I was in a service when the pastor's wife walked a very elderly man with severe asthma up to the front row and asked me to pray for him. I found out he had a badly damaged heart. This guy was on his way out! What was I supposed to pray? I said to myself, **Well, maybe God will give him a new heart.** I prayed for him that night, but had to leave town before the end of the conference.

A few days later a friend called me, really excited. "Do you remember the eighty-year-old with the bad heart and asthma? Well, he's got a new heart! Last night he was dancing on the stage and running around the room, telling us about his new heart!"

On a recent plane flight, as I was thinking about what has happened to me, I suddenly realized I am a sort of "first fruits" of this revival. I think I was the first major healing in Toronto. The inheritance of this revival is healing, and I am walking in that inheritance. This realization has caused a new level of faith and authority to rise in me. It has been over eleven years, and I'm still growing in this! I believe we are going to see more healings, and more profound healings.

I'm 64 now and travel regularly in twelve countries, mostly in Europe. How have all these doors opened up? The Holy Spirit touches one in Switzerland, and she tells her friend in Cologne, Germany. Then I get invited to share in churches and in "church around the kitchen table." It keeps multiplying beyond me. A woman I prayed for in Holland was healed of leukemia. Now she's a missionary overseas.

I have a **burning** in me to see people passionate about life and in love with Jesus, especially the young people. I am seeing so much fear and depression healed. I think I've been given much ministry to youth because they are so preoccupied with death, and that breaks my heart.

I just got back from Germany, where God opened doors to minister to refugees from Kyrgyzstan. One of the pastors saw a deaf woman healed and asked me, "Can God do that for me, too?" I prayed for this deaf pastor, and God healed him, too! The most awesome thing was going back into the Bavarian forest and finding people with an incredible hunger and humility. Ignited for Jesus, they are now eager to go into their own communities.

I once thought of what I'm doing now as something only leaders and pastors and their wives could do. But God is using me, and it's a lot of fun! This revival is about grabbing hold of what God has spoken for you. It's about not saying, "Oh no, not me," but saying, "Let the glory fall!"

Twenty years ago I was ready to die. Now I'm more full of life and joy than I've ever been. I have a great sense of security in my Father. He loves me! The words Randy spoke over me are the message of my life and the message I carry: "Church, you've been sad long enough!"

Seeing with the Eyes of God

The only thing "little" about a "little ole me" is one's perception. And mankind's perception is certainly not God's perception! In the rotting, smoldering dumps of Maputo, in the disease-ridden floodplain of the Zambezi River, in the slums, in abandoned fields still littered with mines, the Bakers' Iris Ministries finds the "least of these"—little ones discarded, unwanted and forgotten by the world. Their own families see no value in them, except perhaps as a body that can be sold on the streets. Many in the West see them as a burden to the earth's resources, better to never have been born. How we need the eyes of God! Truly He is *El Roi*, the God who sees (see Genesis 16:13). He sees past the damage inflicted by the sins of man, and He sees past the work of the enemy—for He sees according to His promise, through eyes of love.

God changes our perception of ourselves and of others, and He empowers us to see as He sees—along with giving us the power to do as Jesus did and even greater things, to glorify the Father. And no matter who we are or where we come from, no matter whether we hold an "important position in ministry" or sit in the back of the Church as a "little ole me," nobody is safe from being clothed with power from on high. Though the pattern is for God to powerfully touch the forceful types who "take the Kingdom by force," there are many exceptions to the pattern. If you are a "little ole me," you may be one of them!

Part 4

Restoring the Lost Doctrine of Impartation

Do not neglect your gift, which was given you through a prophetic message when the body of elders laid their hands on you.

~ *1 Timothy 4:14*

Therefore let us leave the elementary teachings about Christ and go on to maturity, not laying again the foundation of repentance from acts that lead to death, and of faith in God, instruction about baptisms, the laying on of hands, the resurrection of the dead, and eternal judgment.

~ *Hebrews 6:1–2*

9

The Heritage of the Saints

Impartation and Visitation

Unfortunately, we live in a church culture that places little value on the rich heritage of the historical Church. This is the day of the New and Now, where changes and advancements in every area of our lives bombard us at such a pace that we are left hard-pressed to remember yesterday (rotary dial phones?), much less the last century. As a result, we tend to look at today's moves of the Holy Spirit through the tiny peephole of the present, instead of through the telescopic lens of history. Our history is a wonderful story of how God has moved among His people throughout the entire Church Age.

It is our history that provides a proper context and brings clearer understanding to us about what is going on around the world at this very moment. Instead of looking at the current renewal movement as something aberrant and strange, a departure from what is "normal" for God, we will see in the pages to come that God has *often* chosen to invade His people with the glory of His manifest presence. From the days of the early Church fathers to the Dark Ages to the Age of Reason to the present, we see a time line marked by the footprints of Jesus, Emmanuel, as He has walked among us revealing Himself, refreshing the remnant and restoring power and vitality to His Bride.

As we look back at our lineage of saints, I hope to show that the signs and wonders and other phenomena that many believers today consider to be outside the realm of orthodox Christianity have really always been a part of what God intended for His Church. When Jesus promised the Holy Spirit, He never put a time limit on the fullness of the Spirit's presence. When Paul explained the gifts the Spirit gives, he never said they were only temporary gifts. If all the gifts and resources of heaven were necessary to the first Christians, how are the last Christians supposed to bring in the final, great harvest without them? Why would we expect God to equip His people with "power from on high" at the start of the race, and then leave them to crawl, weak and empty, across the finish line?

I do not believe Jesus is coming back for a lukewarm, impotent remnant that has just barely made it to the end, hoping to get raptured before their faith is tested. Rather, I believe we are only just beginning to see the most powerful move of God yet. Jesus is coming back for a radiant, majestic Bride clothed in works of righteousness done in the power and name of the One who does not change!

The Early Church Fathers

Cessationist doctrine teaches that not all the gifts of the Holy Spirit are operative today, and that the "manifestation" and "power" gifts died out with the last of the original apostles and are no longer needed now that we have the complete canon of Scripture. The following excerpts that demonstrate otherwise are taken from the writings of the Ante-Nicene fathers, those who wrote before the Council of Nicea in AD 325. These were the disciples of the first disciples; the first generation of leaders after the apostles had died. Their ministries of healing and deliverance give testimony to the fact of the Spirit's miraculous working in that time.

Throughout early Church history, these gifts of God's manifest power were not "emotional esoteric experiences," as some charge against the signs and wonders we see today. They were core elements of the Gospel these disciples preached, for they preached a gospel of salvation to the whole man. They preached a Jesus full of compassion, who cared about the sickness of a man's body as well as his soul. They preached a Jesus who cared about people's captivity to demonic beings, as well as their bondage to sin. In short, they preached Good News!

Justin Martyr (100–165; martyred in AD 165)

Justin Martyr wrote in his "apology" addressed to the Roman emperor:

> For numberless demoniacs throughout the whole world, and in your city, many of our Christian men exorcizing them in the Name of Jesus Christ . . . have healed and do heal, rendering helpless and driving the possessing devils out of the men,

though they could not be cured by all the other exorcists, and those who used incantations and drugs.[1]

Writing about the charismata, the gifts God pours out on believers, Justin Martyr called attention in several places to the power to heal as one of the particular gifts that was being received and used in the Church.

Hermas (died around AD 150)

From the Shepherd of Hermas, one can see the strong emphasis that was on the ministry of healing in the early Ante-Nicene Church. Hermas wrote, "He therefore, that knows the calamity of such a man, and does not free him from it, commits a great sin, and is guilty of his blood."[2]

Of this, Morton Kelsey comments in his book *Healing and Christianity: A Classic Study*,

> Indeed the healing of physical illness was seen in this period as telling evidence that the Spirit of Christ was actually present and at work among Christians. Since both bodily and mental illness were a sign of domination by some evil entity, the power to heal disease was prime evidence that the opposite spirit—the Spirit of God—was operating in the healer. Thus the healing of "demon possession" was often spoken of in conjunction with curing illness from other causes.[3]

Tertullian (AD 160–225)

In a telling protest written to the proconsul in North Africa during the persecutions there, Tertullian wrote:

> The clerk of one of them [the Roman officials], who was liable to be thrown upon the ground by an evil spirit, was set free from his affliction; as was also the relative of another, and

the little boy of a third. And how many men of rank (to say nothing of common people) have been delivered from devils, and healed of diseases! Even Severus himself, the father of Antonine [the emperor], was graciously mindful of the Christians; for he sought out the Christian Proculus, surnamed Torpacion, the steward of Euhodias, and in gratitude for his having once cured him by anointing, he kept him in his palace till the day of his death.[4]

Healing was simply a fact of the Christian experience back in those times. Pagan officials could easily check into the veracity of the reports if they felt it was warranted. According to Kelsey, Tertullian "explicitly identified persons who had been healed and testified to their great number and the wide range of physical and mental diseases they represented. Elsewhere he also says that God could, and sometimes did, recall men's souls to their bodies."[5]

Origen (AD 185–254)

Concerning Origen, Kelsey writes,

Origen wrote his great treatise *Against Celsus* to take pagan thinking apart piece by piece, and here he spoke in several places of how Christians "expel evil spirits, and perform many cures"—many of which he had himself witnessed. Or again, "the name of Jesus can still remove distractions from the minds of men, and expel demons, and also take away diseases." Several such statements occur in this work, which was written especially for the intellectual leaders of the pagan community.[6]

Kelsey also commented that Origen described in one of his letters how baptism itself was sometimes the means by which serious illness was cured, and that there were Christians who lived on and gave their lives to the Church because of such an experience.[7]

Irenaeus (flourished around AD 175–195)

Of Irenaeus, Kelsey comments,

> Perhaps the most interesting discussion of healing among the ante-Nicene fathers came from Irenaeus in Gaul, who undoubtedly wrote more freely as he was somewhat removed from the danger of persecution that faced most of these men. In *Against Heresies*, one of his telling points was that heretics were not able to accomplish the miracles of healing that Christians could perform. They did not have access to the power of God and so could not heal.[8]

Unfortunately, these comments later became the basis for the idea commonly taught today that unless one's doctrine is 100 percent correct, any miracles or manifestations of the Spirit cannot be of God, but are demonic at their source. This teaching ignores the fact that God is much more interested in whether or not we are *relationally* correct with Him, than in whether or not we have all our doctrinal ducks in a row. The first disciples were sent out to heal the sick and set the demonized free long before they understood even what we consider the most basic foundations of the Christian faith. Summarizing the power encounters Irenaeus witnessed, Kelsey continues,

> Irenaeus attested to almost the same range of healings as we find in the Gospels and Acts. All kinds of bodily infirmity as well as many different diseases had been cured. Damage from external accidents had been repaired. He had seen the exorcism of all sorts of demons. He even described the raising of the dead. His pagan readers were well aware of these

miracles of healing, as he makes clear, since this was often their path to conversion.

There is *no indication* that Irenaeus *viewed any disease as incurable or any healing as against God's will.* Indeed, the whole attitude he voiced was that *healing is a natural activity of Christians as they express the creative power of God, given them as members of Christ. . . . In one place Irenaeus speaks of the prayer and fasting of an entire church as effective in raising a person from the dead* [emphasis added].[9]

It is important to note that Irenaeus was writing primarily to refute the Gnostic heresies of his day. Why is this important? Many famous healers of the Pentecostal/charismatic tradition in this century have been accused of being influenced by Gnosticism—the claim of having a special understanding or revelation of Scripture and esoteric insight into "hidden" knowledge. Yet the "secret knowledge" of Gnosticism taught a distinct separation of matter and spirit. Matter is evil; spirit is good. Therefore, what happens in the realm of the flesh, whether it be sickness or immorality, is of no importance. Because this teaching devalued the natural body, assuming God was not interested, there was no value placed on the ministry of healing. The Gnostics simply did not believe in it. The ministry of Christ's compassion had no place in Gnosticism. How ironic that those accused of Gnostic influence today are actually ministering in direct contradiction to basic Gnostic assumptions!

Further historical testimony to the Spirit's ongoing gifts can be found in the writings of Theophilus of Antioch (died around 181), Arnobius and Lactantius from near the end of the Ante-Nicene period (300–325) and Quadratus, one of the earliest apologists, who wrote in Rome that the works of the Savior had continued to his time and that the continued presence of men who had been healed left no question as to the reality of physical healing.[10]

Augustine (AD 354–430; a Post-Nicene doctor of the Church)

Augustine was the undisputed theologian in the West for a thousand years. His influence is very important to the history of healing. In his early years of ministry, he wrote critically of healing:

> These miracles are not allowed to continue into our time, lest the soul should always require things that can always be seen, and by becoming accustomed to them mankind should grow cold towards the very thing whose novelty had made men glow with fire.[11]

However, about forty years later he corrected this view that seemed antagonistic toward the ongoing ministry of healing in the Church. In his last and greatest work, *The City of God* (completed in 426), he wrote a whole section that gave high value to the ongoing ministry of healing. In it, he noted that over seventy healings had been recorded in his own bishopric of Hippo Regius in two years. After the healing of a blind man in Milan, Augustine wrote, "and so many other things of this kind have happened, even in this present time, that it is not possible for us either to know of all of them or to count up all of those that we have knowledge of."[12]

Later, Augustine's writings would have a tremendous impact on reformers Martin Luther and John Calvin. Augustine's strong views of predestination and God's sovereignty would change the view of the Church from the historic "warfare worldview" to a "blueprint worldview." The warfare worldview looked at the consequences of sin's curse as the work of the enemy, whom the Church had the authority and power to come against. In that historic view, the Church was to continue the work of Christ, who came "to destroy the devil's work" (1 John 3:8).

In the blueprint worldview, though, Christians began to see all things as foreordained and to passively accept what they believed to be God's will. Ultimately, this would have a very negative impact on the theology of healing in the Church. For the sake of historical accuracy, it is important to remember that before Augustine died, he became known for the healing anointing and the authority to deliver that flowed through his own life.[13]

What Happened?

Looking back over the first four hundred–plus years of Church history, the early fathers were collectively saying, "Miracles have not stopped, but still occur today!" Why, then, do we have such division within the Church today on this issue? How did the Church, which witnessed so much healing its first thousand years, become so closed and skeptical toward this vital ministry? I believe we have erred by focusing the redemption we have in Christ totally on the future, with only moral changes in this present life. I contend that this was not the understanding of the early Church. It believed in a present power not only for moral change, but also for authority over demons, power over sickness and disease and experiencing the reality of the spiritual gifts in people's lives, especially in the corporate life of gathered congregations.

Granted, this book is about the doctrine of impartation and anointing, but in directly addressing this issue, we need to understand the validity of what that anointing is *for*! Does God still anoint people to move in signs and wonders? When we see ministries of miraculous healing, deliverance, even the raising of the dead, can we be sure this is truly of God? What about meetings where there is a tangible sense of the supernatural and we witness all manner of emotional and physical responses? Can this be the work of the Holy Spirit? Much of mainstream Christianity to Europe and North America today would answer no. But the majority of Christians in Asia, Africa and Latin America would answer yes!

Again, historical context is important to our understanding of how the Church has been influenced in her interpretation of Scripture. I deal with some of this just ahead in chapter 11, "Building Bridges so Others Might Receive," but in this book, I can only give a brief summary of our theological history since the topic would fill another entire book. (Those interested in learning more, however, can find in-depth materials and referrals to other excellent resources on our Global Awakening website.)

Reformation and Reason

Prior to the Reformation, in the 1200s, Thomas Aquinas had already begun to adopt an antisupernatural theology. Western civilization had crumbled, decimated by corruption, anarchy and epidemic disease. Cities were empty. Education had collapsed. Death and despair permeated all of society. People lost hope for any good in this life, and their spiritual emphasis shifted from the concerns of this life to a focus on the next.

Aristotelian philosophy became the basis for rising Arab culture. In this context, Aquinas wrote most of his *Summa Theologica*, intended as an apologetical work appropriate for the Arabs. Attempting to be relevant to their philosophical mindset, Aquinas shaped his work as a synthesis of Christian and Aristotelian thought.[14] It was a theology based on the senses and the ability to reason, which left little room for the supernatural as it pertained to earthly life. Aquinas's writing became the benchmark of Church theology for the next several hundred years.

Interestingly, at the end of his life Aquinas changed. He had a supernatural encounter with God and wrote on December 6, 1273, *"I can write no more. All I have written seems so much straw compared with what I have seen and what has been revealed to me"* (emphasis added). Three months later he died on a mission trip for the Pope, and others had to finish his book.[15] We will never know what Aquinas might have written had he lived long enough to process his experience into his theology.

The Reformers

On October 30, 1517, Martin Luther nailed his 95 *Theses* to the door of the Wittenberg Church in Germany, and the Reformation "officially" began. Neither Luther nor Calvin ever challenged the Aquinas-Aristotelian synthesis in their writings. Ironically, Luther prayed for his fellow reformer and systematizer of Lutheran doctrine, Philip Melancthon, to be healed when he was near death—and he was healed. Luther also had a gift of faith that resulted in a friend and colleague being healed. In 1540, Lutheran reformer Friedrich Myconius (1490–1546) was sick and about to die. The following passages give us more insight into how Luther prayed for his sick friends. Instead of a "Thy will be done" prayer, I find a "my will be done" in his words. How interesting! I fear that too few Lutherans are aware of this side of Luther's ministry. The following occurred on July 2, 1540:

> Melancthon was on his way to the scene of these delibera-tions when, brooding over this unhappy affair, his fears and scruples brought on a sickness just as he had reached Weimar, which laid him nigh to death's door. Intelligence of his state was conveyed to Wittenberg, and Luther, in the Elector's car-riage, hastened to Weimar. He found Philip, on his arrival, apparently all but dead; understanding, speech, and hearing had left him, his countenance was hollow and sunk, his eyes closed, and he seemed in a death-like sleep. Luther expressed his astonishment to the companions of his journey, "How shamefully has the devil handled this creature!" and then, according to his custom, turning to the window, he prayed with all his might. *He reminded God of his promises from the Holy Scriptures, and implored him now to fulfill them, or he could never trust in them again.* (Emphasis mine, and also note how much this sounds like the prayer of a "Word of Faith" minister.) Rising from prayer he took Melancthon's hand, and called to him in a cheerful tone, "Take heart, Philip: you shall not die. God has reason enough to kill you, but 'He willeth not the death of the sinner, but rather that he should repent and be saved.' He desires life, not death. The greatest sinners that ever lived on earth—Adam and Eve—were ac-cepted of God in his grace; far less will he give you up, Philip, and let you perish in your sins and faintheartedness. Give no room to despondency: be not your own murderer; but throw yourself on your Lord, who killeth and maketh alive." At these words Melancthon evinced a sudden restoration, as though from death to life; he drew his breath with energy;

and after a while turning his face to Luther, implored him "not to stay him; he was on a good journey; and nothing better could befall him." Luther replied, "Not so, Philip, you must serve our Lord God yet longer." And when Melancthon had gradually become more cheerful, Luther, with his own hands, brought him something to eat, and overruled his repugnance with the threat, "Hark, Philip, you shall eat, or I excommunicate you."

The beginning of the next year Luther's intimate friend Myconius seemed rapidly sinking in a consumption, and wrote the Reformer word that he "was sick, not for death, but for life;" but Luther prayed fervently that "Myconius might not pass through the veil to rest, whilst he was left out-of-doors amid the devils," and wrote to his friend that he felt certain his prayers would be heard, and by God's mercy his days would be lengthened, so that he would be his survivor. Myconius was raised up again from the brink of the grave, and eventually outlived Luther seven weeks.[16]

The ending of Luther's actual prayer said, "Farewell dear Frederick. The Lord grant that I may not hear of your departure while I am still living. May he cause you to survive me. This I pray. This I wish. *My will be done.* Amen. For it is not for my own pleasure but for the glory of God's name that I wish it"[17] (emphasis added).

While looking for the quote from Luther's prayer for Myconius, I discovered a very interesting book written in 1832 called *The Suppressed Evidence: Or Proofs of the Miraculous Faith and Experience of the Church of Jesus Christ in All Ages* by Rev. Thomas Boys, M.A., of Trinity College, Cambridge.[18] It appears to me that it gives evidence for the fact that even the Reformers themselves believed in miracles and the possibility of miracles occurring in their time.

Both Calvin and Luther felt keenly compelled to challenge the authority of the Roman Catholic Church. I admit my summary is greatly oversimplified, but their reasoning went like this: "Since the Catholics are using healings to validate false traditions, the healings must either be false or the work of the devil."

The reformers cried out for a return to the objective authority of Scripture, and in the process, they became quite anti-supernatural. It is not hard to understand the animosity of the reformers and why they so vehemently threw out anything that might bolster what they considered a grossly illegitimate claim to spiritual authority. Simply remember the horrors of the day, done in the name of God. Protestants were being viciously persecuted, tortured and burned at the stake by a religious organism that had long lost touch with the Word of God.

In the same period, a group called the Anabaptists appeared on the scene. They were having subjective, revelatory experiences of prophecy. Calvin and Luther felt that this further threatened and undermined a return to the authority of Scripture, especially when those prophecies did not line up with the Word.

The Age of Reason

Alongside this perceived need to reject the supernatural came the Age of Reason. The scientific revolution of the 1700s and 1800s in Europe profoundly affected the Church's interpretation of Scripture. Skepticism flourished toward anything that did not have a material, natural explanation falling within the limits of human comprehension and logic.

These two forces—the cessationism of the Reformers and the scientific skepticism, especially post-Darwin in the Age of Reason—coupled to radically change the landscape of theology regarding present-day supernatural works of God. "Higher criticism," which explained away all the miracles of the Bible in natural terms, first arose in German seminaries. Within fifty years, a rejection of the supernatural for today was taught in most U.S. seminaries. By the late 1800s, it was widely taught that even biblical "miracles" never happened. "Right Reasoning" was on the throne, taking precedence over divine revelation and experience. If it could not be explained, it did not happen.

Fundamentalism came on the scene as a backlash to liberal theology, yet it only addressed the issue of biblical inerrancy and inspiration. Neither liberals nor fundamentalists had a theology of the miraculous, particularly of healing. Fundamentalists viewed the miracles of the Bible as something that were needed only for that time to confirm and establish a new message. Once the Gospel had been "kick-started" and codified in Scripture, miracles were no longer necessary.

It is interesting that in regard to the gifts of the Holy Spirit today, Pentecostals have more in common with Roman Catholics than they do with other Protestants, for the Roman Catholics have never been cessationist in their doctrine. John Wimber once told me that those who have the hardest time receiving healing are certain Protestants, while those who receive the easiest are Roman Catholics, as they are more open to the miraculous.

The Road Back to Pentecost

From what has been covered so far, it might sound as if the Church went for centuries without any faith in or practice of the supernatural gifts of the Holy Spirit. That is far from the case. Evangelicals began seeing healing in the mid-1800s. From 1875 until 1900, healing was the most controversial subject of many denominations. This was before the rise of Pentecostalism at the beginning of the 1900s; God was revealing Himself in supernatural power in the midst of the most conservative, mainline denominations. It is a little-known fact that many of today's cessationism-teaching churches were birthed in renewal movements marked by charismatic manifestations. It is only the widespread ignorance of Church history that has cut so many of us off from our spiritual roots.

First Great Awakening/Jonathan Edwards

In 1735, revival broke out in the American colonies through the ministry of Jonathan Edwards in what became known as the First Great Awakening. Jonathan Edwards is the preeminent theologian on religious experience. To this day, no one has written a more thorough and reasoned discussion of the subject. I have read that he was one of the greatest thinkers of America. He was the best defender of the Great Awakening. His wife was so touched in the revival that she would be overcome for hours by the Spirit of God. On one occasion she was experiencing a powerful visitation that lasted the better part of four days. Look at some of the accounts of this revival:

> Wednesday night, the church in Northampton was hosting protracted revival meetings. Mrs. Edwards was so filled with the grace of God that it "took away her bodily strength." She writes: "I *continued* to have clear views of the future world, of eternal happiness and misery . . ." She and some friends had to stay at the church about three hours after the meeting

was dismissed, because most of the time, her "bodily strength was overcome . . ."[19]

It is interesting that at least one modern-day chronicler of these events notes that the expressions "took away her bodily strength," "overbear the body" and "fainting" that were used at the time seem to be eighteenth-century equivalents to our twentieth-century expressions of "falling," "resting" and being "slain in Spirit."[20]

The following morning, Mrs. Edwards was again overcome by the presence of God. When she accidentally went into a room where some people were discussing the reviving work of the Holy Spirit, her strength was "immediately taken away" and she "sank down on the spot." Those present propped her up on a chair and continued to converse, and "again her strength failed her, and she dropped to the floor." They then put her to bed, where she lay "for a considerable time faint with joy, while contemplating the glories of the heavenly world. . . ." Mrs. Edwards related that during this time, she "felt a far greater love to the children of God, than ever before. I seemed to love them as my own soul; and when I saw them, my heart went out towards them, with an inexpressible endearedness and sweetness. . . . This was accompanied with a ravishing sense of the unspeakable joys of the upper world." She was out that day from noon until four, "being too much exhausted by emotions of joy" to even rise or sit up.[21] By late afternoon she had enough strength to go to the evening meeting, then she returned to bed.

Mrs. Edwards continued to have similar experiences of God's empowering and joyful presence throughout the revival. She records her experiences for seventeen days, and there is no indication that these types of experiences discontinued during the revival. Rather, she discontinued writing about them. What was the fruit of these experiences for Sarah Edwards? Mr. Edwards marked a new and deeper spirit of worship in his wife, along with an increased sense of how the duty of every Christian was to show charity to the poor. In all that Mrs. Edwards experienced, her husband commented that there was no appearance of spiritual pride in her, but instead a great increase of meekness and humility, and a desire to prefer others, along with a great aversion to being judgmental.[22] Here are some of his final words of assessment about her condition:

> Now if these things are enthusiasm, and the fruits of a distempered brain, let my brain be evermore possessed of that happy distemper! If this be distraction, I pray God that the world of mankind may be all seized with this benign, meek, beneficent, beautiful, glorious distraction![23]

Those critical of revival accused people who were thus affected by it of having distemper of the brain, and *enthusiasm* was at the time a negative term intended to disparage the adherents of revival. It is difficult, however, to be a detractor of a move of the Spirit when your wife has been powerfully touched by that move of God. Edwards was asking his critics what better way there was to see the outworking of Scripture than through the present manifestations that were accompanying the revival. However, *he always judged whether the manifestations were from God not by the degree of the manifestation, but rather by the fruit that followed.* Edwards believed there was little power in religion that did not affect the emotions and will. Religious affections were the driving power of Christianity. Only when the revelation of divine truth went deep enough to touch the affections did this divine truth then have power to affect the will and lifestyle of the believer. The Holy Spirit had to work through our affections, not just our understanding or our knowledge.

Edwards noted the difference in character and fruit between the members of his church prior to the revival and those touched in the revival. Again, Edwards was always looking for fruit. More than any other person in America, he carefully studied the relationship between bodily manifestations and fruit, between the internal working of the Spirit and the outward manifestations upon the physical body of these internal workings.

What did these manifestations look like? How were they described? The following are some terms Edwards used to describe the phenomena: *extraordinary affections* that were accompanied by physical manifestations of fear, sorrow, love and joy. *Tears, trembling, groans, loud outcries, agonies of the body and the failing of bodily strength. Fits, jerks and convulsions.*[24]

Why have I chosen to include these insights from the Great Awakening, which was called the "Great Clamor"[25] by its critics while it was occurring, especially since the subject of this book is impartation? Because I believe revival itself has the characteristic of being spread through impartation. Sometimes the impartation is for a vision/understanding of what God is presently doing—that the season of refreshing has begun. Sometimes the impartation comes through reading an account of what God is doing in another area or hearing the testimony of others who have been touched in the fresh outpouring. Other times it comes by seeing it firsthand, and other times by being touched in the meetings or by having hands laid on you by the leader of the meeting or being prayed for by one of the leaders of the move of God.

During the Awakening he found himself leading, Edwards noted the following:

> There were *many instances* of persons who came from abroad on visits, or on business, who had not been long here before . . . they were savingly wrought upon; and partook of the shower of blessing which God rained down here, and went home rejoicing, *till at length the same work began evidently to prevail in several other towns in the country* [emphasis added].[26]

This impartation for carrying revival can be seen in the First and Second Great Awakenings, the Holiness Revival of the nineteenth century and the Pentecostal Revival at the beginning of the twentieth century. It was also present in the greatest revival in Baptist history in Shantung Province of northern China in the 1930s, the Latter Rain Revival and the Healing Revival of the late 1940s, the charismatic renewal both of Protestantism and Catholicism, as well as in the Jesus movement and Third Wave movement of the 1960s, '70s and '80s respectively. I also saw it in the move of God connected to Rodney Howard-Browne, myself and John Arnott, John Kilpatrick and Steve Hill, Steve Gray and others in the 1990s. In fact, Rodney Howard-Browne's prophetic insight about impartation for carrying revival encouraged me to go see him and receive prayer from him multiple times. God had told him that he "would lay hands on a thousand pastors who would help take revival around the world." I believed in the truth of impartation, and I asked to be one of the thousand.

Wesley and Whitefield

Let's return to our historical perspective by moving from the Great Awakening in the American colonies to the work of God in England. Just prior to this revival in North America, the Great Evangelical Revival had already broken out in England under the ministries of John Wesley and George Whitefield. Wesley, the founder of Methodism, witnessed demonic deliverance in his meetings, as well as people being thrown to the ground—later called "swooning," and later still, "slain in the Spirit." Note what Wesley wrote in this series of excerpts from his journal in the year 1739:

Thur. [March] 8.—[. . . One] who sat at a small distance, felt, as it were, the piercing of a sword, and before she could be brought to another house, whither I was going, could not avoid crying out aloud, even in the street. But no sooner had we made our request known to God, than he sent her help from his holy place.[27]

Tues. [April] 17.—. . . Immediately one that stood by (to our no small surprise) cried out aloud, with the utmost vehemence, even as in the agonies of death. But we continued in prayer, till "a new song was put in her mouth, a thanksgiving unto our God." Soon after, two other persons (well known in this place, as labouring to live in all good conscience towards all men) were seized with strong pain, and constrained to "roar for the disquietness of their heart." But it was not long before they likewise burst forth into praise to God the Saviour.[28]

Sat. [April] 21.—At Weaver's Hall a young man was suddenly seized with a violent trembling all over, and in a few minutes . . . sunk down to the ground.[29]

Thur. [April] 26.—. . . Immediately one, and another, and another sunk to the earth: They dropped on every side as thunderstruck.[30]

Mon. [April] 30.—We understood that many were offended at the cries of those on whom the power of God came: Among whom was a physician, who was much afraid, there might be fraud or imposture in the case. To-day one whom he had known many years, was the first (while I was preaching in Newgate) who broke out "into strong cries and tears." He could hardly believe his own eyes and ears. He went and stood close to her, and observed every symptom, till great drops of sweat ran down her face, and all her bones shook. He then knew not what to think, being clearly convinced, it was not fraud, nor yet any natural disorder. But when both her soul and body were healed in a moment, he acknowledged the finger of God.[31]

Tues. May 1.—. . . A Quaker, who stood by, was not a little displeased at the dissimulation of those creatures, and was biting his lips and knitting his brows, when he dropped down as thunderstruck. The agony he was in was even terrible to behold. We besought God not to lay folly to his charge. And he soon lifted up his head, and cried aloud, "Now I know thou art a prophet of the Lord."[32]

These were the accounts of sinners and religious detractors who were knocked down to the ground, slain in the Spirit. Revivals are often accompanied by such phenomena. It is difficult for us to accept that God's Spirit would cause people to be thrown to the ground, but in Scripture when there is a theophany (a visible manifestation of God), most of the time the people become afraid, sometimes they fall and other times they tremble.

The greatest evangelist of the Great Evangelical Revival was George Whitefield. He began leading this revival in 1735 at the young age of 21. He was concerned about some of the phenomena he was hearing about in the reports of John Wesley's meetings. Wesley wrote in his journal about a discussion he had with Whitefield regarding this:

> Sat. [July] 7.—I had an opportunity to talk with him of those outward signs which had so often accompanied the inward work of God. I found his objections were chiefly grounded on gross misrepresentations of matter of fact. But the next day he had an opportunity of informing himself better: For no sooner had he begun (in the application of his sermon) to invite all sinners to believe in Christ, than four persons sunk down close to him, almost in the same moment. One of them lay without either sense or motion. A second trembled exceedingly. The third had strong convulsions all over his body, but made no noise, unless by groans. The fourth, equally convulsed, called upon God, with strong cries and tears. From this time, I trust, we shall all suffer God to carry on his own work in the way that pleaseth him.[33]

George Whitefield, the greatest evangelist of the Great Evangelical Revival, also experienced healings in his meetings. He wrote, ". . . and I trust, the Sun of Righteousness arose on some with healing in His wings. The people were melted down very much at the preaching of the Word . . ."[34] The amazing thing revealed in Whitefield's journals was the repeated statements about George being weak in body, often very ill, and God coming in power with the preaching of the Word.[35] There were accounts of deliverances, but no accounts of George praying for divine healing with the laying on of hands. Healing in this phase of Protestant history was still a lost doctrine, only to be rediscovered by the later Holiness movement, then by the Faith Cure movement that included Reformed, Baptist and Christian & Missionary Alliance people, along with writers from beyond these denominations (such as Anglican and Episcopal), and then by the Pentecostal people.[36]

When reading the journals of Wesley and Whitefield, one cannot help but think of how Jesus rebuked the Pharisees of His day for honoring the prophets when their actions toward Him indicated that, had they lived when the prophets lived, they would have stoned them rather than honored them. It is amazing how we honor today those who were ridiculed and maligned during their ministries. The lesson of history is that it is easy to be favorable toward renewal or revival from the safe distance of time, but hard to be open to participating in the "Great Clamor"—the label by which the Great Awakening was originally known.

Wesley and Whitefield would be considered "counterfeit revival leaders" if they were conducting their ministry today. They would be guilty of participating in the false "slain in the Spirit movement." They would definitely be accused of emphasizing esoteric experiences and hyping their meetings. Recordings of some of their meetings would be played over the radio, especially with the more bizarre aspects featured, such as screaming, wailing, weeping, roaring and those other things that often occurred in their meetings. Because their meetings were accompanied with enough power to cause the affections (emotions) to be moved upon by the Spirit of God, could it be possible that these very phenomena were what attracted the attention of the English and American people of that day?

What was the fruit of the Great Awakening in the colonies of America? Whitefield was drawn to America eleven times, and he died in the colonies. Was it real revival, or was it people just getting caught up in esoteric experiences? Decide for yourself:

> In one period of three years during the awakening, at least thirty thousand persons were converted in New England. And in the same period at least fifty thousand persons were converted in all the colonies. When one remembers that the total population of the colonies was about two million, these numbers are no less than amazing. A similar awakening today would have to result in more than five million conversions to achieve the same percentage.[37]

Second Great Awakening

The Second Great Awakening began to gain steam around 1792, when God began to visit colleges. By 1800, many churches in the United States were experiencing revival, with the most famous of those meetings being the Cane Ridge Revival in Kentucky.[38]

Ironically, the Cane Ridge Revival came out of a tradition that originated with the Scottish Presbyterians. The Presbyterians had a prolonged communion service that would take place once a year and last for three to five days. There had been five or six such meetings in Scotland where the "fire fell" or where God would "light the fire again." The "wild meetings," as they were called, began in Ulster and peaked around 1724. "It was in these Ulster communions that we first have reports of people fainting dead away and being carried outside in a trance."[39]

The largest and most famous of the Scottish meetings was held at Cambuslang. Estimates ran as high as thirty thousand people in attendance. George Whitefield had just returned from one of his trips to America, and he preached with great passion and anointing. Historian Paul Conkin writes,

> Small groups of people, under deep conviction, talked all the night. Whitefield preached the thanksgiving sermon on Monday, after which people were reluctant to leave. No one could estimate the number of converted. Almost every conceivable physical exercise, including falling in a swoon, afflicted some participants. The ministers deplored disruptive behavior during the services, but in spite of their appeals many cried out, even during communion, and in later interviews swore they could not control themselves however much they tried. . . . But in these three or four waves of revival, the huge rural gatherings, with all the extreme physical exercises, dismayed or frightened possibly a majority of Presbyterian clergymen. . . . Cambuslang was the focus of much of the controversy. Within nine years at least fifty-eight books, plus endless articles, either praised or condemned it.[40]

The local pastor, McCulloch, developed a questionnaire to assess the effects of the revival and defend what had happened. "The effects on the local congregation were lasting, although the revival ebbed very quickly. Conversions continued until 1748, but with annual decreases. Crimes all but ceased in the immediate aftermath, but not for long. Approximately four out of five converts remained in the church for the next decade."[41] For those who question the fruit of such renewal experiences, we might compare this to today's retention rate of 6 percent from crusade evangelism after just one year. The Cambuslang renewal produced a retention rate of 80 percent after ten years!

The same controversy that swirled around Cambuslang resurfaced when the Cane Ridge Revival hit. What was this revival like? James B. Finley was a Methodist circuit rider who was among the thousands converted during this move of God. Finley wrote,

> The noise was like the roar of Niagara. The vast sea of human beings seemed to be agitated as if by a storm . . . The scene that then presented itself to my mind was indescribable. At one time I saw at least five hundred swept down in a moment, as if a battery of a thousand guns had been opened upon them and then immediately followed shrieks and shouts that rent the very heavens.[42]

Although Cane Ridge did not originate with the Baptists, it was part of what became known among Baptists as the Awakening of 1800. Dr. Lewis Drummond, co-author of *How Spiritual Awakenings Happen*,[43] stated in his lectures on evangelism at The Southern Baptist Theological Seminary that because of this revival, the Presbyterians doubled, the Baptists tripled and the Methodists quadrupled. But often, when God pours out His Spirit division results. The Presbyterians would be split into two denominations due to the Cane Ridge Blessing. It was too much for some, so it was rejected by them.

Peter Cartwright

One of the great Methodist leaders of the 1800s was Peter Cartwright. He had been touched in the Cane Ridge Revival and was soon converted and called into the ministry. During the early days of Methodism in this country, it is reported that many young Methodist circuit riders did not marry because they knew that about 50 percent of their number died before reaching the age of 30. Peter Cartwright was one of the courageous early circuit riders and one of their most famous evangelists of that era. From his autobiography, he speaks,

> Many nights, in early times, the itinerant had to camp out, without fire or food for man or beast. Our pocket Bible, Hymn Book, and Discipline constituted our library. It is true we could not, many of us, conjugate a verb or parse a sentence, and murdered the king's English almost every lick. But there was a Divine unction attended the word preached, and thousands fell under the mighty hand of God, and thus the Methodist Episcopal Church was planted firmly in this Western wilderness, and many glorious signs have followed, and will follow, to the end of time.[44]

What a powerful, honorable history of the Spirit the Methodists have! Cartwright also wrote about the Cumberland Revival that soon followed Cane Ridge:

> The Predestinarians of almost all sorts put forth a mighty effort to stop the work of God. . . .
>
> Just in the midst of our controversies on the subject of the powerful exercises among the people under preaching, a new exercise broke out among us, called the jerks, which was overwhelming in its effects upon the bodies and minds of the people. No matter whether they were saints or sinners, they would be taken under a warm song or sermon, and seized with a convulsive jerking all over, which they could not by any possibility avoid, and the more they resisted the more they jerked. If they would not strive against it and pray in good earnest, the jerking would usually abate. I have seen more than five hundred persons jerking at one time in my large congregations. Most usually persons taken with the jerks, to obtain relief, as they said, would rise up and dance. Some would run, but could not get away. Some would resist; on such the jerks were generally very severe.[45]

Cartwright's interpretation of these phenomena is worthy of noting:

> I always looked upon the jerks as a judgment sent from God, first, to bring sinners to repentance; and, secondly, to show professors that God could work with or without means, and that he could work over and above means, and do whatsoever seemeth to him good, to the glory of his grace and the salvation of the world.[46]

Charles Finney Spreads the Fire

Charles Finney was the greatest revivalist of the 1800s in America. Some say he was the greatest American evangelist of all time. His biography is filled with power encounters that he experienced and witnessed. Just hours after his conversion, he experienced a mighty baptism in the Holy Spirit. This sovereign "impartation" from heaven would radically change his life. He describes his experience this way:

> Without any expectation of it, without ever having the thought in my mind that there was any such thing for me, without any recollection that I had ever heard the thing mentioned by any person in the world, the Holy Spirit descended upon me in a manner that seemed to go through me, body and soul. I could feel the impression, like a wave of electricity, going through and through me. Indeed it seemed to come in waves and waves of liquid love for I could not express it in any other way. It seemed like the very breath of God. I can recollect distinctly that it seemed to fan me, like immense wings.
>
> No words can express the wonderful love that was shed abroad in my heart. I wept aloud with joy and love; and I do not know but I should say, I literally bellowed out the *unutterable* gushings of my heart. These waves came over me, and over me, and over me, one after the other, until I

recollect I cried out, "I shall die if these waves continue to pass over me." I said, "Lord, I cannot bear any more" yet I had no fear of death.[47]

After this experience, the first person Finney spoke to went to get an elder. The elder came to help Finney because Finney had been so wiped out by the power of the experience. This elder of the church was a serious and grave man but, as Finney was telling him how he felt, the elder fell into a "most spasmodic laughter. It seemed as if it was impossible for him to keep from laughing from the very bottom of his heart."[48]

Finney received a second impartation from heaven, which he called the baptism in the Spirit, within 24 hours of the first, and then began to preach the day after his conversion.[49] He would have many baptisms in the Spirit. His controversial ministry would see thousands falling under the power of the Holy Spirit, with healings, deliverances, shakings, groanings and weeping. Some who fell under the power would not be able to get up for long periods of time. In an era of sparse population and no media, Finney would be used to bring half a million people into the Kingdom of God!

Phenomena have been very much a sign of the power of God in revivals. Often, these phenomena also produce controversy and division within the churches. It is sad that when these things are written up later, our church historians often sanitize the accounts of the meetings, removing the supernatural dimension. When several Southern Baptist seminary professors of evangelism were asked by phone, "What was the greatest revival in Baptist history?" the response was unanimously, "The Shantung Revival in China."[50] Healing, falling, electricity, laughing in the Spirit, even raising the dead are recorded in *The Shantung Revival*, a book by Mary

Crawford that I mentioned in chapter 3. Crawford was one of the Southern Baptist missionaries who experienced this revival firsthand in the early 1930s. In her book are accounts of almost everything that has been characteristic of the Toronto Blessing and the Pensacola Outpouring. Unfortunately, most Southern Baptists are not aware of what happened during their greatest revival because several years ago Crawford's book was reprinted with almost all of the phenomena of the Holy Spirit edited out. Global Awakening has republished this book with its entire original content.[51]

Pentecostal Revival

Revival ushered in the 1900s, just as it had the 1800s. The Frontier Revival, or Second Great Awakening, was followed by the even more powerful Pentecostal Revival, which dates back to 1901. Again we would see people falling, shaking, rolling, weeping, wailing, dancing, laughing in the Spirit and speaking in tongues. The uniqueness would be that, for the first time, tongues were tied to the baptism in the Holy Spirit as the initial evidence.

Azusa Street would occur in 1906. The first name for the Azusa Street Revival was the "Los Angeles Blessing."[52] Hungry people would travel to it from every inhabited continent to find more of the manifest presence of God and then return to spread the Pentecostal Revival in their countries. Participants believed in impartation, the transference of anointing, and were empowered to carry the revival back to other places. Like the Latter Rain Revival of the 1940s, this revival emphasized the return of all the spiritual gifts of 1 Corinthians 12, including the "sign gifts" of tongues, interpretation of tongues, prophecy, working miracles and gifts of healings.

It is disappointing to me how much prejudice still exists in the church toward Pentecostals. When I was taking a course on evangelism in seminary, we studied every revival in North American church history except four: the Pentecostal Revival; the Latter Rain Revival, which was a Pentecostal revival in its origin; the Charismatic Renewal; and the Jesus Movement, which had just ended.[53] It is shameful that these revivals are not even mentioned in our evangelical seminaries and colleges.[54] It is not healthy to allow our prejudice to blind us to the facts of how powerfully God has used Pentecostals. In their early days, when they had no institutions, buildings, money or programs, they were used to reach more lost than any other part of the church—more than the Reformed, the Lutheran, the Anglican, the Baptist, the Methodist and the Roman Catholics. These denominations, with all their history, buildings, finances, organization and programs, were surpassed in evangelism by the Pentecostals.

Why? The Pentecostals embraced the outpouring of the Holy Spirit's power and the restoration of the power ministries of the Holy Spirit as still being operative for today. *Sozo*, the Greek word for *save*, is used in the Bible to refer to not only the saving of the soul, but to deliverance from demonized situations and to physical and emotional healing. It was the Pentecostals' understanding of the fullness of our salvation that gave such spiritual power to their message.

Pentecostalism was preceded by leaders like Charles Spurgeon (1834–1892) who were looking for the restoration of a fully empowered, apostolic Church as seen in the days of the first Pentecost. Spurgeon was a Calvinist, yet he had a healing ministry and moved in words of knowledge during his services. He prophesied a great move of the Holy Spirit within the next fifty years after he was speaking. It was in those next fifty years that we saw the birth of the Holiness movement, spearheaded by some of this century's giants of the faith, A. J. Gordon, A. B. Simpson and Andrew Murray. These men would also be leaders in the Faith Cure movement.[55] These renewal movements emerged from within several existing denominations, as there was no "Holiness" church in existence at the time.

The Holiness movement emphasized a second work of grace following initial regeneration. The purpose of this second experience was a "filling" with the power of the Holy Spirit that enabled the believer to experience sanctification—practical victory in his daily experience, not just positional victory in the spiritual realm and in the life to come. It was a return to the doctrine of "Christ is Victor," which was the prevailing understanding of the cross of Christ during the first six hundred years of Church history.[56] In short, it means we understand that the cross did not just secure our ultimate salvation, but that all of Satan's power was met head-on and defeated, breaking the dominion of the curse. The death of Jesus was certainly a "substitutionary atonement," but the scope of what He did goes far beyond that. By His death and resurrection, and ascension, Jesus conquered all the powers of hell. Because of His victory, Christians may walk in authority and power over death in all its forms—spiritual, emotional and physical.

Out of this return to historic *Christus Victor* theology came the Faith Cure movement. This movement would be eclipsed in about 25 years by the birth of the Pentecostal movement. With the great disdain of evangelical Protestants for the Pentecostal movement, which embraced healing, there was a reaction by evangelicals away from the Faith Cure movement into an even stronger cessationist position.

I often hear the phrase, "I'm not concerned with phenomena; what I'm concerned about is evangelism." Can there be any question that the mightiest moves of the Spirit, those that have resulted in the greatest number of people coming to God, have been those times of revival characterized by powerful outpourings of spiritual gifts and manifestations of God's very presence? It is also clear from Church history that most of these leaders first received their own impartation of the Spirit prior to accomplishing such powerful things in Jesus' name. Men and women like Maria Woodworth Etter, John G. Lake, Smith Wigglesworth, Charles Price, F. F. Bosworth, Aimee Semple-McPherson, Tommy Hicks, Lester Sumrall, T. L. Osborne, Oral Roberts, Kathryn Kuhlman, Reinhard Bonnke, Benny Hinn, Bill Johnson, Rolland and Heidi Baker, Ché Ahn, John Arott, myself and a host of others all received a powerful impartation from God before they were powerfully used of God.

Other men like A. J. Gordon, Andrew Murray, A. B. Simpson, E. W. Kenyon, A. T. Pierson, D. L. Moody and R. A. Torrey also testified to having received the baptism in the Holy Spirit. These men were less connected to entering the healing movement through an impartation. Like the late John Wimber, they saw healing in the Bible and wanted to be faithful to the Bible, and in doing so began teaching on healing. Their impartation was more for evangelism, and their approach to healing was based on the promises of Scripture.[57]

What about Today?

When we see men and women who claim an anointing of God to move in signs and wonders, healings and deliverance, and when we see ministries accompanied by all manner of phenomena, can we know it is of God? We have certainly seen the historical impact of men and women used in the past and the fruit of earlier outpourings of the Spirit. What about more recent times?

Like many streams flowing into one great River of God, the 1940s brought the revival ministry of William Branham in 1946, the Sharon Orphanage revival of 1947, the Healing Revival of 1948 and the evangelistic ministry of Dr. Billy Graham in 1949. Although diverse in nature, I do not believe these were separate moves of God, but rather one great outpouring that manifested in a variety of ways. Since then, I believe we have been accelerating toward the greatest revival of all, the last harvest before the return of Jesus Christ for His Bride.

I see the great River of God of the 1990s revival in a similar manner. There was Claudio Freidzon in 1992, Rodney Howard-Browne in 1993, John Arnott and myself in 1994, John Kilpatrick and Steve Hill in 1995 and Steve Gray in 1996. Many others were also used in these periods of revival both in the 1940s and the 1990s, but space and time do not allow us to mention them all.

In this last decade, evangelists like Benny Hinn and Reinhard Bonnke have preached to millions in one place. I was in India the same time Benny Hinn was ministering to over a million souls. My crowds were from 25,000–100,000 per night. What drew the people? The miracles of God?

What about evangelist Dr. Billy Graham? He does not move in miracles, so does his success invalidate my arguments? I think not. About 25 years ago, I was studying about people being filled with the Holy Spirit. I read that when Dr. Graham was up in the mountains of California near a lake, he had an experience with God where there was a more complete surrender to the purposes and power of God for his life. This experience happened shortly before his famous Los Angeles meetings in 1949, where he gained national notoriety. Three years earlier, Stephen Olford led Dr. Graham into an experience of being filled with the Spirit.[58]

So many men and women have been powerfully anointed by God to bring about revival through the various giftings of the Spirit. They are being used *right now* to change the world.

In the next chapter, we will consider how the Lord brought His Church back from the brink of almost losing her understanding about how important impartation and the gifts of the Spirit are. It took a full-blown, massive recovery effort orchestrated by the Holy Spirit, with the results so important to God that He caused both Protestants and Roman Catholics to begin praying for a "new Pentecost." This is one of the most amazing stories in the history of the Church. Once you see what God purposed to do and then what He effected in His Church, you will see a much bigger picture of how important this "new Pentecost" was to the heart of God.

10

Winds of Change

Preparation for Restoration

During the time of Charles Finney's ministry in America, God was also working in the hearts of many evangelicals in England. A great expectancy was building during the 1800s regarding the fulfillment of end-time prophecies. Prior to the outbreak of the Civil War in the United States, the prevailing end-time view was postmillennialism, which taught that Jesus would return after the Church had successfully established the Kingdom of God on the earth and had taken the Gospel to all nations. Many believers held a popular view that, as Jesus' appearing came closer, the Church should expect a great end-time revival where the earlier "sign gifts" of 1 Corinthians 12 would be restored to the Church.

After the Civil War, a dispensational pre-Tribulation rapture theory became the most popular view in the United States regarding the end times. This view was predisposed to deny an end-time revival or the restoration of the sign gifts, and although it was popular in the United States, it had only a small impact on European Christians. For hundreds of years the Church, both Catholic and Protestant, had not expected the average person to be able to move in the gifts of healing, working of miracles, prophecy, tongues and interpretation of tongues. Other gifts like words of knowledge and words of wisdom were redefined to remove their supernatural aspect. Sometimes prophecy was also treated in this manner and was considered the equivalency of preaching. This was the classical Calvinist interpretation and was also a view strongly held by the Lutherans. But by the last half of the 1800s, this view was changing to a rising expectancy in Europe for the restoration of the gifts and offices of apostolic Christianity.

Daniel 7 and Revelation 13 were key prophetic passages that many believed were in the process of being fulfilled during the late 1700s. Vinson Synan, dean of Regent Divinity School and the most famous Pentecostal church historian of the twentieth century, wrote,

> As the French Revolution unfolded, biblical scholars were certain that these passages were literally being fulfilled. The introduction of a new "revolutionary" calendar and the installation of a prostitute in Notre Dame Cathedral as a newly crowned "Goddess of Reason" seemed to underscore the apocalyptic event of 1798 when French troops under General Berthier marched on Rome, set up a new republic, and sent the Pope into exile. This was seen as the "deadly wound" marking the end of papal hegemony in the world.[1]

A student of biblical prophecy interpreted the 1260 years mentioned in Revelation and the "times, times, and half time" in Daniel to be from the year 538 (the end of the Goths' rule in Rome) to 1798 as the fulfillment of the prophecy. Synan continues,

> To Protestant scholars this interpretation meant they were living in the very last days. The second coming of Christ was near; the millennium was shortly to begin; the Holy Spirit would soon be poured out upon all flesh as a further sign that the end was near. The long night of waiting was almost over. *At any time the charismata would again be manifested in the earth as on the day of Pentecost* [emphasis added].[2]

Evangelicals in England and on the Continent continued to expect an end-time outpouring of the gifts of the Spirit. In 1857, Charles H. Spurgeon, a famous Baptist preacher, gave a sermon titled "The Power of the Holy Spirit." In it, he said,

> Another great work of the Holy Spirit, which is not accomplished is the bringing on of the latter-day glory. In a few more years—I know not when, I know not how—the Holy Spirit will be poured out in far different style from the present. There are diversities of operations; and during the last few years it has been the case that the diversified operations have consisted of very little pouring out of the Spirit. Ministers have gone on in dull routine, continually preaching—preaching—preaching, and little good has been done. I do hope that a fresh era has dawned upon us, and that there is a better pouring out of the Spirit even now. For the hour is coming, and it may be even now, when the Holy Ghost will be poured out again in such a wonderful manner, that many will run to and fro and knowledge shall be increased—the knowledge of the Lord shall cover the earth as the waters cover the surface of the great deep; when His Kingdom shall come, and His will shall be done on earth as it is in heaven. . . . My eyes flash with the thought that very likely I shall live to see the

out-pouring of the Spirit; when "the sons and the daughters of God shall prophesy, and the young men shall see visions, and the old men shall dream dreams."[3]

Growing Hunger in the U.S.

In the United States, the emphasis on the restoration of the gifts of the Spirit, and on receiving an experience of the Holy Spirit subsequent to conversion, was moving from the fringes of the Church to its center. This was becoming more visible, especially during the last 25 years of the nineteenth century. The emphasis within the Holiness movement had been primarily the Methodist viewpoint that power for sanctification or holiness was a "second definite blessing." This was now becoming a dual message where the "second blessing" included the Holy Spirit's gifts of power.

The Keswick movement was a more Calvinistic movement and was represented by such men as the Baptist A. J. Gordon and Presbyterian A. B. Simpson. But one of the strongest leaders in this new emphasis on a subsequent experience of power was D. L. Moody, founder of the Moody Bible Institute. Then came R. A. Torrey, Moody's successor and a president of Moody Bible Institute, to carry the torch. Moody's Northfield Conferences became a major impetus to the teaching of a "baptism in the Holy Spirit" for power.

Moody would die in 1899—just before the outbreak of the expected and much sought after, much prayed for "new Pentecost." These Northfield Conferences in Massachusetts were the meetings where E. W. Kenyon was tremendously influenced in the formation of many of his theological views. His greatest source of quotes is from the Baptist A. J. Gordon.[4]

Kenyon would later influence the man who brought the "finished work" teaching to the Assemblies of God denomination in its formative years. This finished work teaching influenced Holiness teacher Phoebe Palmer, who emphasized confessing what the Word of God taught concerning your sanctification until you possessed it.

Simpson, Gordon, Andrew Murray and Kenyon would all apply this same approach to physical healing—confess the truth of God's Word based on the finished work of Christ until the possession of the reality is yours. This was the message of the Faith Cure movement in the last quarter of the nineteenth century. It was picked up by the new Pentecostal denominations, and later, healing evangelists like T. L. Osborn would express their indebtedness to Kenyon, who was representative of this teaching. F. F. Bosworth's book *Christ the Healer* (Revell, 2001) is a summation of the Faith Cure movement's conclusions.

Some were also expecting the restoring of the offices of the prophet and the apostle to the Church, not just the gifts of healing, miracles, tongues and interpretation of tongues. In the 1830s a man by the name of Edward Irving, a famous Presbyterian pastor in London who saw people in his church experience tongues, prophecies and other gifts, believed that God had restored the gifts of apostles and prophets. He was excommunicated by the Presbytery as a heretic for such a belief. Some time later he died a broken man in disgrace.[5]

One of the saddest notes associated with the answer to a century of prayer for the Pentecostal outpouring was its rejection by some of the very groups that had cried out for just such a visitation and restoration of the gifts. Perhaps it was because of the way it came at Azusa Street. In the day of

Jim Crow laws and the segregation of the races, the idea that God would choose a one-eyed black man with little formal education as the instrument of the revival, and would locate it in a former livery stable on the wrong side of the tracks, was more than many could handle. It seems that God likes showing up in stables.

Phineas Bresee, the head of the newly formed Pentecostal Church of the Nazarene denomination, had himself received a powerful impartation at the occasion of his sanctification. (*Sanctification* here is the Holiness movement expression that refers to a powerful work of grace in the life of the individual that frees the person from the power of sin. This was a powerful, emotional experience that was definite and that followed the conversion experience.) Yet Bresee rejected the Pentecostal message and removed the Pentecostal name from the denomination. However, Bresee did describe receiving an extremely powerful impartation from God:

> I sat alone in the parsonage, in the cool of evening, in the front parlor near the door. The door being opened, I looked up into the azure in earnest prayer, while the shades of evening gathered about. As I waited and waited, and continued in prayer, looking up, it seemed to me as if from the azure there came a meteor, an indescribable ball of condensed light, descending rapidly toward me. As I gazed upon it, it was soon within a few score feet, when I seemed distinctly to hear a voice saying, as my face was upturned towards it: "Swallow it; swallow it," and in an instant it fell upon my lips and face. I attempted to obey the injunction. It seemed to me, however, that I swallowed only a little of it, although it felt like fire on my lips, and the burning sensation did not leave them for several days. While all of this of itself would be nothing, there came with it into my heart and being, a

transformed condition of life and blessing and unction and glory, which I had never known before. I felt like my need was supplied. I was always very reticent in reference to my own personal experience. I have never gotten over it, and I have said very little relative to this; but there came into my ministry a new element of spiritual life and power. People began to come into the blessing of full salvation; there were more persons converted; and the last year of my ministry in that church was more consecutively successful, being crowned by an almost constant revival. When the third year came to a close, the church had been nearly doubled in membership, and in every way built up.[6]

Jesus said, "I will build my church, and the gates of hell shall not prevail against it" (Matthew 16:18, KJV). Jesus does not belong to the Vineyard movement, nor to any other new apostolic network. Neither is He a Roman Catholic, a Baptist, an Assembly of God member or a Nazarene. He is the pioneer of our faith, the original Christian, the "anointed one." It has been said that God does nothing without first setting His Church to pray—then He responds to the prayers. God definitely set His Church to pray in preparation for the greatest release to His Church in seventeen hundred years or more, or maybe even since the first Pentecost!

Roman Catholic Stirrings

Now that we have addressed this restoration within Protestantism, let me share what was being done within the Roman Catholic Church in preparation for the new Pentecost. This is an amazing story of grace from within the Roman Catholic Church. In the next few pages, I am drawing entirely on the material from Monsignor Walsh's book *What Is Going On? Understanding the Powerful Evangelism of Pentecostal Churches.*[7]

In his book, Monsignor Walsh tells of how God moved powerfully within the Catholic Church, causing it to pray for a new Pentecost. He believes that the Catholic Church contributed to the Pentecostal revival through its prayers, joining as well with the prayers of many Protestants. He relates the story of Blessed Elena Guerra (1835–1914), the first person beatified by Pope John XXIII, who founded a religious congregation dedicated to spreading devotion to the Holy Spirit (The Oblate Sisters of the Holy Spirit). She formed prayer groups she called "Pentecost Cenacles," hoping that "Come, Holy Spirit" might become as popular a prayer among Catholics as the Hail Mary. She advocated 24-hour prayer cenacles, hoping the Catholic Church would be united in constant prayer, as were Mary and the apostles. In 1885, she felt called to write to the Pope but resisted until many years later. Then between 1895 and 1903, she wrote twelve confidential letters to Pope Leo XIII, each calling for renewed preaching on the Holy Spirit.

Pope Leo (papacy 1878–1903) published *Provida Matris Caritate* (The Provident Charity of a Mother) in response to Elena's letters. In it, he asked for a solemn novena between the Ascension and Pentecost throughout the Church. This was not enough, Sister Elena prodded, so he wrote his famous encyclical on the Holy Spirit, *Divinum Illud Manus* ("That Divine Gift"). The encyclical was excellent, though the response of the Church was poor.

Possibly even more important than the encyclicals, however, at the insistence of Blessed Elena, Pope Leo dedicated the twentieth century to the Holy Spirit, invoking on January 1, 1901, the "Veni Creator Spiritas" ("Come, Holy Spirit") upon the whole world. I think this is extremely interesting because that very day, January 1, 1901, marked the first time tongues as the initial evidence of the Holy Spirit's baptism occurred in Topeka, Kansas, with students in Parham's Bible school.

Monsignor Walsh relates another series of events that took place in a small village in Czechoslovakia. Back in the eleventh century, when the village faced starvation because of crop loss due to severe cold, a beautiful lady appeared on the mountain there. She never identified herself, but taught the villagers to call on the Holy Spirit. Following her teaching, they were filled with the Holy Spirit and manifested all of the Pentecostal gifts, including healing, prophecy and tongues. The villagers avoided starvation that winter because the bread they had baked was multiplied, and the supply miraculously held out until the next harvest.

Each successive generation of villagers manifested the same charisms. The village needed neither a jail nor a hospital, so strong were the power of prayer and God's presence there. When someone was sick, the whole village united in prayer— and they expected God to heal. Divorce was nonexistent, and families welcomed every child God sent. Children were taught to live in the power of the Spirit. The Bible was read in each home. On Sundays, they all joyfully celebrated the Mass and shared a fellowship meal.

Through the prophetic word in the 1930s, the villagers were told that a severe testing would empty the village. This prophecy was fulfilled in 1938, when the Nazis killed almost everyone. During the executions, the Holy Spirit gave the villagers perseverance. Not one renounced his or her faith due to the threats.

Mrs. Anna Mariea Schmitt was a surviving member of that small village, as well as a survivor of both Nazi and Russian concentration camps. Hers was a remarkable parish totally immersed in the Holy Spirit for nine centuries. And amazingly, this charismatic village was visited many times by Bishop Angelo Roncalli, later Pope John XXIII. Anna Mariea loved to sit at his feet and listen to him teaching about Jesus. He was completely at home amidst the openly charismatic manifestations he saw there. Anna Mariea was once asked if she thought Pope John's prayer for a new Pentecost was inspired by her village. She thought, however, that his desire for a new Pentecost was in his heart long before he visited them. He seemed to know what could happen when people invoked the Holy Spirit.

Monsignor Walsh relates, "When Angelo Roncalli became the Pope [in 1958] and called the Second Vatican Council, he asked the whole Church to say a special prayer which began, 'Renew your wonders in this our day, as by a New Pentecost.'"[8] He also adds that in the early days of the new Pentecostal movement, they constantly thanked Pope John, knowing that the new movement would not have been accepted without his Council. Pope John XXIII died in 1963. Four years later, as a total surprise of the Spirit, the Catholic Pentecostal Renewal began. Monsignor Walsh commented that those involved would say to each other, "If only Pope John knew what would happen because of his prayer for a New Pentecost."[9]

According to Monsignor Walsh, although two important popes of the twentieth century openly sought the fire of the Holy Spirit on the Catholic Church (both Leo XIII and John XXIII), sadly, for the most part the signs and wonders that were happening took place outside the Catholic Church. As a result, in some countries thousands were drawn away from Catholicism into places where they could experience more of the Holy Spirit. Monsignor Walsh concludes,

> In all honesty, Pope John seems to have been pushed into the background, as if his Pentecostal dream was too naïve. If we don't awaken soon, we will discover that the Pope's Pentecostal dream was all too true, but we were not open to the fire of the Spirit.[10]

Are We Ready?

The Roman Catholic Church petitioned God for another Pentecost at the turn of the century and then again in the 1960s, but still could not embrace the Spirit when He came. This was the response of the majority of the Protestant Church as well. The Roman Catholic Church relegated the new presence of the Spirit to special groups outside their regular worship service, the Mass. In like manner, while many traditional Protestant denominations allowed "closet charismatic" fellowships of pastors and leaders to form, they did not dare to bring the new dynamic of the Spirit into their normal worship services. They, too, relegated the Spirit to special events and groups, but did not welcome the new Pentecost into regular Sunday worship. The result was that those who wanted to experience the fullness of the Spirit in corporate gatherings—not just in some small group hidden from the rest of the congregation—left to start or join new charismatic churches where this freedom was permitted.

Many feel a need for the graces and gifts of the Spirit to be ordered by the formal rituals of the Church. In this way prophecy has been reduced to ritualistic charges given at ordination. The laying on of hands has become a ritual to set people into their place of service. The call of laborers is no longer from the Lord through the prophets of the Church, but comes through the wisdom of the nominating committee and the vote of the congregation. For too many, the local church is no longer functioning as a theocracy where God is in control, but as either a pure democracy where the majority vote wins the decision or as a republican form of government where representatives from the congregation lead it through a session, a leadership team or whatever term is used.

The problem with this form of church life is that it has lost the sense of the presence of God leading, guiding, sustaining, calling, supplying and visiting. Little wonder that no mystery is left in church meetings! I am afraid that Rev. Dave Gernetsky, pastor of the largest Baptist church in South Africa at the time (Quigney Baptist Church in East London in 1998), was right when he said to me, "We pray for the Holy Spirit to come, but when He does, the first thing we tell Him is, 'Now sit down on the back seat and behave Yourself.'"

Impartations are wonderful, but they are also messy. They can be loud and disruptive to the "ritual" when they occur. When God comes to visit His Church in revival or renewal, He will behave in a manner true to who He is—He *does* think He is the Head of the Church. When He comes, He comes to take over, not to sit in the backseat and conduct Himself in such a way that it pleases the majority of the people. The Rev. Gernetsky, who once had been reluctant to allow the Holy Spirit free rein in his church, also said to his congregation, "I don't aim to be disrespectful, but when we were praying for God to come, our prayers were like, 'Here kitty, kitty, kitty,' and *Rooaaaaarrrrr*, the Lion of Judah showed up! He was so much stronger and fiercer than the tamed, controllable 'kitty' we were expecting."

As C. S. Lewis said about the lion Aslan, a type of Christ in his THE CHRONICLES OF NARNIA, He is good, but He is not safe!

I am afraid this move of God that came to the Church in the 1990s and quickly spread around the world was rejected largely because of the tension between man and God for control of the liturgy or order of the service. It seems to me that every major revival of the twentieth century involved God attempting to restore His control over the Church in an experiential way, not just in a theological or doctrinal understanding of this reality. Almost every one of these moves emphasized the restoration of the gifts of the Holy Spirit and a return to the use of the words *apostolic* and/or *Pentecostal*. Likewise, through these moves the Church saw a new order of men and women arise who were sent out (which is the basic meaning of the word *apostolic*) as missionaries or as new preachers of the Gospel, and people experienced a new vibrancy in Church worship. This was true for the initial Pentecostal outpouring with Parham in Topeka, Kansas, in 1901, and it continued in the Welsh Revival of 1904, the Pentecostal Revival of Azusa Street in 1906, the revivals in the 1920s and 1930s under Smith Wigglesworth and a host of other Pentecostal healing evangelists, the 1947 Latter Rain Revival, the 1948 Healing Revival, the charismatic renewal of 1960s, the Jesus movement of the late 1960s and early 1970s, the Third Wave movement of the 1980s and the "Laughing Revival" of the 1990s.

Impartation has been a powerful tool of the Holy Spirit in the spreading of each of the moves of God around the world. I know that the Toronto Blessing was only a part of the "Laughing Revival," as some have called it, but through Toronto alone, over 55,000 churches were touched by the Spirit in just the first year. Millions of people came to what began in a little storefront church at the end of an airport in Toronto.

The most amazing thing about the Toronto Blessing was how *transferable* it was. One newspaper article in London likened it to the Beijing flu.[11] How was it transferred? Primarily through the laying on of hands, often accompanied with prophecy. It is still being transferred around the world today—but it is only being transferred and received in those places where people are willing to allow God to take control and lead His Church. Perhaps one of the reasons impartation has become the most forgotten and most neglected "elementary teaching" of the New Testament Church is because, through prophecy and the laying on of hands, God is in the driver's seat, so to speak, of the local church and the Church at large. He appoints, He calls, He empowers, He sends to the nations and He truly is leading His Church. Church is no longer a safe place to visit. You can no longer set your clock by the liturgy when God runs things by His Spirit.

In this new millennium, we Christians no longer find ourselves in a predominantly Christian culture. We now find ourselves in a pagan culture in much of the world. We find more similarities in our culture to the first two centuries after the crucifixion and resurrection of Jesus than at any other time. If the Church is to be the leaven that leavens the whole lump, if we are to see the Kingdom of God ever expanding, then we will not be able to trust in our might or power, but must rely on the Spirit of God. "'Not by might nor by power, but by my Spirit,' says the LORD Almighty" (Zechariah 4:6). We need to recapture all the elementary teachings listed in Hebrews 6:1–2, including the one most lost in the history of the Church—the laying on of hands.

I agree with Pope John Paul II, who in his major encyclical *Veritatis Splendor* ("The Splendor of Truth") reaffirmed the importance—even the necessity—of the working of the Holy Spirit unbound from the rationalistic approaches of our day, free to do His work in the "new evangelism":

> At the heart of the new evangelization and of the new moral life which it proposes and awakens by its fruits of holiness and missionary zeal, there *is the Spirit of Christ*, the principle and strength of Holy Mother Church. As Pope Paul VI reminded us: "Evangelization will never be possible without the action of the Holy Spirit." . . . As Novatian once pointed out—here expressing the authentic faith of the Church—it is the Holy Spirit "who confirmed the hearts and minds of the disciples, who revealed the mysteries of the Gospel, who shed upon them the light of things divine. Strengthened by his gift, they did not fear either prisons or chains for the name of the Lord; indeed they even trampled upon the powers and torments of the world, armed and strengthened by him, having in themselves the gifts which this same Spirit bestows and directs like jewels to the Church, the Bride of Christ. It is in fact he who raised up prophets in the Church, instructs teachers, guides tongues, works wonders and healings, accomplishes miracles, grants the discernment of spirits, assigns governance, inspires counsels, distributes and harmonizes every other charismatic gift. In this way he

completes and perfects the Lord's Church everywhere and in all things."[12]

Ralph Martin, key renewal leader and writer within the Roman Catholic charismatic movement, then proceeds to make an insightful analysis that has parallels for Protestants. He states:

> I remember when the contemporary manifestations of the charismatic renewal first broke out in the Catholic Church in 1967 some theologians opined that the charismatic gifts of the Spirit were really not necessary in the twentieth century since they were given to the early Church because she lived in the hostile environment of a pagan society and needed such manifestations of the Holy Spirit to confirm the preaching of the gospel.
>
> I hope it is clear from the previous chapters and the witness of our own experience that we are no longer living in a Christian society and that we need all the "power from on high" that we can get. How rapidly Christendom is dissolving before our eyes! How rapidly one age of Church history is ending and another is beginning! How much has changed in the last twenty-five to thirty years! How quickly we are again coming to the situation the early Church was in as she lived her life and preached the gospel in the midst of a pagan society. How desperately we need a new Pentecost![13]

I want to finish here by adding that this new Pentecost, this restoration of the gifts of the Spirit, must also include a restoration of all the dimensions of the lost doctrine of the New Testament Church. And it must include the one elementary teaching most stolen from the Church by the devil—the doctrine of the laying on of hands, which included an understanding of the impartation both of the gifts of the Spirit and of the Holy Spirit Himself. Why has the devil fought so hard against this doctrine? Because of its power to bless the Church. For this reason, the devil fights by using misunderstanding and division within the Church to stop the restoration of the ministry of impartation. Until this doctrine is fully restored to the Church, she will not be able to claim that all grace is at work in her.

11

Building Bridges so Others Might Receive

In these pages, you and I have explored together the biblical foundation for the doctrine of the laying on of hands, and we have looked at the winds of change that have ushered in revival. You have also heard my testimony of receiving an impartation and how it revolutionized my life and ministry. Through the testimonies of others who have received "power from on high," we have also seen the fruit of impartation all around the world. There are still those, however, who have major issues with impartation. They face obstacles in their viewpoints and beliefs that keep them from desiring an impartation. One of my goals in writing these pages is to help remove these obstacles and to build a bridge of understanding that will allow these people to come out of the land of skepticism and unbelief regarding the present-day ministry of the gifts of the Holy Spirit.

Back in 1994, I heard the still, small voice of the Lord speak to me ever so clearly, "You are to be a fire lighter, vision caster and a bridge builder." I understood the "fire lighter" to mean facilitating outbreaks of the presence of God in power in certain areas or churches. I knew being a "vision caster" would involve lifting up people's understanding toward believing God for great things—miracles, healings, deliverances and powerful manifestations of His presence in their midst. And I came to understand that being a "bridge builder" dealt with bridging the gap for people by removing the barriers that were keeping them from entering into the full blessings of God through the power of the Holy Spirit. Additionally, bridge building dealt with building relationships between key leaders around the world to bring greater unity between them for the purposes of revival.

The task of building a bridge from the world of the Pentecostal/charismatic/third-wave evangelical to the world of the cessationist evangelical over the great gap of misunderstanding and mutual skepticism is not an easy one. In order to build this bridge of understanding between these two camps, it is necessary not only to look at the Scriptures, but also to look at historical theology. Historical theology not only considers what the Bible says, but also looks at when an interpretation first arose and whether it has been the predominant viewpoint of the Church.

Let's apply historical theology to some of the major obstacles that prevent those in the cessationist camp from receiving or embracing impartations of the Holy Spirit. The bridge I am attempting to build by looking at these issues is one over which I hope many will be able to cross—into the land of God as the "I Am," where "Jesus Christ is the same yesterday and today and forever" (Hebrews 13:8).

Major Issues with Impartation

What are some of the major issues related to people rejecting the idea of impartation or the transference of the anointing? What obstacles get in the way of them believing in the continuation of all the gifts of the Holy Spirit, and in the continuation of all the offices of the Church as listed in Ephesians 4:11–12? What makes some people so skeptical about most renewal and revival movements, including the Toronto Blessing? I believe there are four basic reasons for this rejection of the idea that the power of the Holy Spirit's gifts is for today:

1. A worldview that came into the Church through Thomas Aquinas in the 1200s, three hundred years prior to the Reformation. Formerly, the perception was that truth and reality come from two sources, the spirit realm (revelation) and reason. This other worldview, however, moved toward the idea that they come from reason alone. Thomas Aquinas was one of the most important theologians of Roman Catholicism, and his *Summa Theologica* caused Christianity to become more rationalistic based.[1]

2. Rationalistic-Enlightenment thinking that developed in the 1700s and continues with us today. It is based on a philosophical presupposition that nothing supernatural can happen. This is most clearly represented in eighteenth-century philosopher David Hume's book *Of Miracles* (Open Court Classics, 1986).

3. The Protestant Polemic (or argument) against the charismata happening after the Apostolic Age. The resulting viewpoint is termed *cessationism*.

4. An understanding of the end of time from a dispensational viewpoint that developed around 1830. This viewpoint takes a defeatist attitude toward the end of time and views the last period of time as a season when the Church is lukewarm, not in revival. It also believes that this weak, desperate, lukewarm Church will be raptured away prior to the end-time tribulation.[2]

I have dealt with most of these issues at some level in this book or in other books, but I would like to say a bit more here about cessationism, the belief that the gifts ended with the death of the apostles or the canonization of Scripture. This topic is vitally important because holding to cessationist beliefs automatically rules out the continued ministry of impartation. This is because impartation often involves the gift of prophecy and the gifts of healings and/or words of knowledge, as well as a fresh filling or baptism in the Holy Spirit.

B. B. Warfield was the most influential cessationist scholar of the last century. He was a famous professor at Princeton Theological Seminary, and in 1917 he wrote the book *Counterfeit Miracles*, which was believed to prove beyond any doubt the case for cessationism. Warfield defended the fundamentals of the Christian faith against the liberal theology of the day. I was told during my college and seminary education that his book *Counterfeit Miracles* drove the last nail in the coffin of the belief that miracles have continued throughout the history of the Church.

Warfield, however, was very inconsistent in his methodology.[3] He misunderstood the primary purpose of the miraculous, and his method of evaluating miracles was inconsistent. In addition, his own hermeneutic for interpreting the Bible, when applied faithfully to the texts of Scripture germane to this discussion, would disprove his cessationist position![4] For a thorough study of cessationism from a philosophical, biblical and historical perspective, see Jon Ruthven's book *On the Cessation of the Charismata: The Protestant Polemic on Postbiblical Miracles*. It provides the best information I have studied on the subject, along with an exegesis of all the major passages related to it and a first-rate analysis of the philosophical presuppositions of cessationism. It also notes in further detail the inconsistent historical method employed by Warfield. Ruthven comments in his book that in Warfield's *Counterfeit Miracles*, "hardly more than half a dozen pages of over three hundred are devoted to this scriptural grounding, and of this, almost nothing in specific exegesis of texts."[5]

Bridging the Gap

If we are to close the divide or bridge the gap for those who are skeptical about impartation and the gifts of the Spirit in operation today, I believe it will need to be done by means of good biblical interpretation, a consistent historical method for the evaluation of miracles and honest reporting on the positive fruit (not just the most bizarre events) connected to renewal and revival movements. On the basis of genuine evangelical, scholarly, radical exegesis of the text, we will find a place to agree.

I believe that whatever camp we are in presently, we all can agree that a world full of lost and hungry souls still needs the God whom we call Savior. Our message to them must not be limited to a God who once empowered His saints for supernatural ministry, but cannot be expected to continue doing for us what He did in the "golden age" of the early Church. Neither can our message be limited to what our God will do in the future, when He comes again. No! Our message needs to be about what our God is able to do in the present for those who are in need *now*.

God loves the world and is trying to reach it through the Church, His Body on earth. The Lord Jesus desires to continue executing His will "on earth as it is in heaven" because He is "the same yesterday and today and forever" (Matthew 6:10; Hebrews 13:8). This means that the purpose of the Father, revealed through the Son, is to be continued by the activity of the Holy Spirit from the time of Pentecost until the Second Coming of Jesus. Everything the Father has belongs to *all* the Church—not just to the Pentecostals or charismatics. It belongs to those who by faith appropriate what has been given by grace.

By way of building bridges, I want to state that those who move in grace-based gifts are not any more holy or any more saved than those who do not. Neither are they more mature in the Lord. They do often see, however, more fruit in the approaching end-time harvest. When we hunger for and experience greater intimacy with God and greater outpourings of the Holy Spirit, it leads us to the places where God's heart is drawn—to the poor, the widows, the orphans and the unregenerate peoples of the world. When we experience God's love and refreshing ourselves, we then arise from His banqueting table and go in new strength to carry His message to the world.

My desire is to see in the Church at large what we see on the short-term missionary teams Global Awakening takes to the nations. The question of what "camp" someone came out of fades away as you realize that you do not know who the Pentecostals are from the Presbyterians on the team, or who the Methodists are from the Mennonites, or who the Catholics are from the Church of God-Cleveland or who the Baptists are from the Brethren. Rather than being divided over past issues and obstacles, we find ourselves loving each other with a quick bonding that can only be supernatural. We have a joyous time together casting out demons, healing the sick and laying hands upon leaders for the impartation of more grace-based gifts. All that matters to the teams is Jesus and seeing Him continue to build His Church through the present-day ministry of the Holy Spirit.

As you and I have explored together in the pages of this book how we can recover the biblical doctrine of laying on of hands, I have attempted to remove the obstacles that have kept many from desiring an impartation. I have attempted to build a bridge of understanding that will allow people to come out of the land of skepticism and unbelief regarding the present-day ministry of the gifts of the Holy Spirit. This bridge is one over which I hope many will cross. As children of God, none of us needs to settle for living our lives like one of the "hired men" when, in fact, the Father wants us by His side at His table, enjoying our inheritance and all that He has for us in the here and now. Run into His arms! Appropriate His grace! Work with Him in power! All that He has is ours.

Conclusion

Living Out Impartation

In summary, let me state that I believe the Bible does not fit either the Pentecostal or the evangelical position regarding the baptism in the Holy Spirit or how one receives other types of impartations. Both positions are too narrow. I believe the same God who made no two fingerprints and no two snowflakes alike did not intend to make our experience of His Spirit the same for everyone.

When we look back at biblical passages, especially those in Acts, we see differences in how believers experienced the Holy Spirit. In Acts chapter 2, we see that people were baptized in/filled with the Holy Spirit at a prayer meeting *with* tongues, while in Acts 4:31 they received the baptism in the Holy Spirit *without* tongues. Sometimes the Spirit came after water baptism, with the laying on of hands and no tongues, as in Acts 8. At other times, such as in Acts 9, we are not told the particulars of how or when someone received an impartation of the Spirit. Impartations of the Spirit can occur at the time of conversion, before water baptism and with tongues and prophecy accompanying them, such as is seen in Acts 10 at the house of Cornelius. Impartations can also occur after water baptism, with the laying on of hands accompanied by tongues and prophecy, as in Acts 19.

A God who likes diversity appears to be at work here, and I suggest that we need to learn to like diversity, too. In fact, I believe that if we could learn to appreciate this biblical diversity, it would enable us to appreciate the diversity within the Body of Christ, a diversity that Satan has previously used to divide us.

In my former church, we honored and welcomed people who had had experiences different from our own that reflected this New Testament diversity. We did not try to convince them that their experience was not valid or not normative. Rather, we emphasized that God is free to baptize us and fill us with His Spirit or to impart gifts to us in whatever way He so chooses. Keeping this in mind, we can find unity in the midst of diversity.

As a matter of fact, my emphasis has been less on the experience of receiving an impartation of the Spirit and more on the fruit of having an intimate relationship with Jesus Christ. The reason I have encouraged the people of my church not to ask someone if they have been baptized in the Spirit is that the answer does not really tell us much. What do I mean? It is like asking people if they have had a wedding. They may answer yes, but that does not tell you anything about their relationship with their spouse. They may be living in marital hell. They may be living in marital bliss. They may now be divorced or widowed or separated. We do not really know much about a marital relationship by asking someone if he or she has had a wedding. Rather, we learn more by asking people how intimate they are with their mate and whether they love their mate more today than when they first got married.

In like manner, people could have had an experience with God years ago—call it baptism in the Holy Spirit or some kind of impartation of the Spirit—but now they are cold or lukewarm or backslidden. Or they may be passionately in love with God. Focus on the *relationship*. In this way people cannot hide behind an experience of the past. It is not enough to have received a baptism in the Holy Spirit; we must continue being filled with the Spirit. It is not enough to have received an impartation of the Spirit; we need to live in the continuing power of the Spirit.

Not only does the Bible reflect people's diversity of experiences pertaining to impartations of the Holy Spirit, but so does the history of the Church. I must believe that Jesus was right in Luke 24:49 when He made the reception of power evidence of the Holy Spirit: "I am going to send you what my Father has promised; but stay in the city until you have been clothed with power from on high." I also believe that Arthur Blessitt was right when he told us we should emphasize the "red"—referring to the words of Jesus in the Bible.

When I read the history of the Church, I find that those who received "power from on high" then exerted a powerful influence on the Church and society. Some of these people, like Francis of Assisi, Ignatius Loyola, Francis Xavier and Mother Teresa, were Roman Catholic. Others like George Whitefield and Dr. Billy Graham were/are Reformed. Others like John Wesley, John Fletcher, E. Stanley Jones and

Charles Finney were Armenians. Still others like Maria Woodworth-Etter, John G. Lake, Smith Wigglesworth, T. L. Osborn, Oral Roberts, Omar Cabrera, Carlos Annacondia, Claudio Freidzon, Luis Palau and David Yonggi Cho were/ are Pentecostals.

I cannot believe that the non-Pentecostals mentioned above were not baptized in the Holy Spirit or had never received an impartation of the Holy Spirit because they did not speak in tongues. Nor can I believe that others were filled who spoke in tongues but had little impact on Church and society. If power is a major purpose and evidence of the presence and work of the Holy Spirit, then I must acknowledge that Church history and the Bible both indicate that people can be baptized in the Holy Spirit or receive an impartation in diverse ways, with diverse experiences.

Dr. Billy Graham concludes his book *The Holy Spirit* with this illustration:

> Over 100 years ago, two young men were talking in Ireland. One said, "The world has yet to see what God will do with a man fully consecrated to Him." The other man meditated on that thought for weeks. It so gripped him that one day he exclaimed, "By the Holy Spirit in me I'll be that man." Historians now say that he touched two continents for Christ. His name was Dwight L. Moody.[1]

The Result Is in the Fruit

For my part, I thank God that He made it possible for me to receive a good education for ministry. I thank God for the Baptists who helped me go through college and seminary and for my seminary class on revivals. Because of these things, I learned so much about historical revivals. Dr. Lewis Drummond's class at the Southern Baptist Theological Seminary prepared me to recognize revival. Those classes exposed me to almost all of the phenomena that occurred in Toronto through my reading about the historic revivals in America.

The greatest revival in Christian history, however, was not talked about in my college and seminary classes. In fact, it was totally ignored. That was the great Pentecostal Revival. God in His providence saw that this was a blind spot for me and removed it from my eyes. He created divine appointments for me to begin to learn about the great revivals of the Pentecostals. Because of these studies, I learned that not too many were saved in the Azusa Street Revival that lasted about three years, yet this was truly a revival. The result was in the fruit—in what happened to the people who came to the meetings. They were baptized in the Holy Spirit, and with this impartation they returned to their region of the United States or the world, where the salvations then began. From these revived churches, or the newly formed Pentecostal churches, would come a world revival accompanied by the greatest missions outreach of the century. In less than one hundred years, Pentecostals and charismatics would become the largest group of Protestant Christians in the world, numbering more than all other Protestants combined. Where other Protestant works have been going for five hundred years, the Pentecostal movement would sweep past them in numbers of adherents, conversions and workers in just a hundred years.

I hope as you read of the revival that has broken out in Mozambique and around the world, you, too, will hunger for the outpouring of God in your own life and in your church. I hope you are hungry for an impartation from God. I hope you will not be afraid of the manifestations of God's Holy Spirit. I hope those who sell fear of these things through their radio program and/or books will not mislead you. These detractors of revival can only see the extremes and paint the moves of God according to these extremes. Furthermore, they only communicate the worst fruit, which occurs when pastors and/or their parishioners do not use wisdom in handling the power of God. We rarely get to hear of the good fruit that results from these moves of God.

In the preceding chapters, you have read about real and lasting fruit. I hope that I have laid out enough of the biblical and historical foundation for what we are experiencing so that it no longer causes fear and rejection. I do not know if it is too late for the United States and Europe to get in on what we have come to call this move of God—the River. The opportunity has come and may now be gone. I hope not. I pray for another visitation of God's presence for our country. This time, I hope there is enough information about true revival and its accompanying phenomena so that people will not respond in fear or fight the move of God, but will instead respond in faith and embrace what God is doing. I hope they will desire to be among the first to receive a fresh impartation of this new thing God is doing.

I hope this book has made you hungry for more—hungry for an impartation of apostolic love and compassion, hungry for an impartation of the gifts needed to be more fruitful in your ministry. I believe you are hungry! Otherwise, you probably would not have bought this book and read it up to this point. I believe God sees your hunger and wants to touch you. I believe some of my readers will become missionaries. Others will become church planters, pastors and key leaders in the Church. It has been my experience that those who have received an impartation are those who are most ready to serve in the Kingdom of God and who have the most joy while serving.

I will be the first to admit that not everyone is called to go to the nations, but everyone is called to go *somewhere*. The question is, where? Perhaps you will be called to a distant land, another nation like Mozambique, Cambodia, Ukraine or Brazil. Perhaps you will be called to go to the slums, to the poorest of the poor, whether in our nation or in another. Some will be called to reach their neighborhoods, their towns or their cities, and some will even be called to minister to the prostitutes on the streets or to the drug addicts. The point is that we are all called to go. Even those of us who give our lives in serving the local church must model this sense of being "sent ones."

If we want to be more successful in our going—to whatever place or whatever group—we need more of the anointing. We need a fresh impartation from heaven. I remind you of the concern of Mel Tari in his council not to lead people into thinking that all they need is someone to lay hands on them so that they receive an impartation. He is right; you need much more than this. You need humility, character and integrity, as well as intimacy with God. What you receive in an impartation must be lived out in faithful obedience, even when it involves suffering. What you receive must be guarded through maintaining a personal relationship with God. You must guard your heart against pride, bitterness, unforgiveness, broken relationships or covenants and the lust for fleshly or material things. Always "seek first His kingdom and His righteousness, and all these things [your needs, not desires] will be added to you" (Matthew 6:33, NASB).

Be Touched and Refreshed

As we conclude, let me pray for you. I advise you to pray the following prayer and then wait upon the Lord to come and touch you. If you find yourself waiting, remember that time goes by slowly when we wait. Some of us have a tendency to wait for only a few minutes, but I counsel you to wait upon the Lord for at least ten minutes. Wait upon Him, and I believe you will be touched and refreshed. You may even receive a commission from God with an impartation so strong that you will become a "history maker in the land."

Father, in the name of Jesus I ask that You would meet the faith and hunger of the person holding this book. I bless this person in the name of Jesus and ask for Your Holy Spirit's fire to come upon him or her. I ask that You would release Your compassion and love into this person's heart right now. I ask that You would especially impart the gifts of word of knowledge, healings, prophecy and the working of miracles through this person in the days ahead. As he or she waits in Your presence, Father, with hands outstretched and palms raised, I ask that Your power would touch these hands. Multiply Your power. Increase Your power. Baptize this reader in Your Holy Spirit, and fill this soul with the peace of the Prince of Peace. In Jesus' name, Amen.

God bless and strengthen you with His mighty power as you begin or continue the exciting ministry of cooperating with the Holy Spirit. Through Him we are enabled to become co-laborers with Christ. Let the name of Jesus Christ be held in high honor in our cities as people witness healing and deliverances, along with the Gospel being shared with power from on high.

Notes

Chapter 1: The Biblical Foundation for Impartation

1. Gordon Fee, *Paul, the Spirit, and the People of God* (Peabody, Mass.: Hendrickson Publishers, 1996), 102–103. Dr Fee also notes on page 84, "What is hard to imagine is Paul ever having such a conversation with his new converts. In Galatians 3:1–5, when he encourages them to stay with 'faith in Christ' and not get entangled with 'works of law,' he first appeals not to the truth of the gospel, but to their experience of the Spirit by which they started on the path of Christian discipleship. This is not an appeal to feelings but to something common to them all—the experienced reality of their conversion to Christ through the coming of the Spirit."

Chapter 2: A Man Made Ready: My Testimony of Impartation

1. For more detailed accounts of my impartation testimony and the fruits that followed, see my other books *Healing Unplugged* (Chosen, 2012), *The Essential Guide to Healing* (Chosen, 2011) and *Lighting Fires* (Global Awakening, 2006).

Chapter 3: How to Receive an Impartation

1. Billy Graham, *The Holy Spirit: Activating God's Power in Your Life* (Waco: Word, 1975), 107.

2. Once out of print, her book was reprinted by our ministry, Global Awakening, in 2005 and is now available on our website. An edited 1970 version left out most of the accounts of manifestations. The Global Awakening edition was a reprint of the original.

3. This concept is prevalent in Lawrence Wood's *The Meaning of Pentecost in Early Methodism* (Lanham, Md.: Scarecrow Press, 2002).

4. Joe McIntyre, *E. W. Kenyon: The Man and His Message of Faith, the True Story* (Orlando, Fla.: Creation House, 1997), 189–210. Kenyon was most influenced by the Baptist A. J. Gordon, who in turn was influenced by the Christian & Missionary Alliance writer George Peck. Peck's 1888 book *Throne Life* had a huge impact on Gordon, and through Kenyon his ideas influenced William Durham. Durham in turn introduced the Finished Work teaching to the early Assemblies of God denomination.

5. Vinson Synan, *The Holiness-Pentecostal Movement in the United States* (Grand Rapids: Eerdmans, 1971), 53.

6. McIntyre, *E. W. Kenyon*, 47.

7. Leaders of the Keswick movement included Robert Pearsall Smith, Reverend Evan H. Hopkin, J. Hudson Taylor and Reginald Radcliffe. It began in 1875 in Keswick, England. You can find more information online at http://online.ambrose .edu/alliancestudies/docs/Keswick_1.htm.

8. Graham, *Holy Spirit*, 108.

9. Ibid., 110 (italics Graham's).

10. Gordon Fee, *God's Empowering Presence: The Holy Spirit in the Letters of Paul* (Grand Rapids: Baker Academic, 2009).

11. See more on this in Wood, *The Meaning of Pentecost in Early Methodism.*

12. Graham, *Holy Spirit*, 110.

13. Ibid.

14. Ibid., 112–113.

15. Harold Lindsell, *The Holy Spirit in the Latter Days* (Nashville: Thomas Nelson, 1983), 111 (emphasis mine).

16. Ibid., 113–122.

17. Ibid., 120.

18. Ibid.

19. Ibid., 121. I do not see any difference in the use of Scripture or approach to Scripture between Lindsell's teaching about being filled with the Spirit and the Word of Faith's teaching about how to receive healing. Though these are two different subjects, the approach is to Scripture and to faith statements being confessed as reality without the experience yet being manifested. I struggle not with the method of appropriating, but with the possibility of being satisfied with a faith confession that has not manifested.

Chapter 6: Why Impartations? Why Signs and Wonders?

1. For a more detailed listing of the various ways God's glory is revealed, see chapter 6, "Healing and the Glory of God," in my School of Healing and Impartation workbook *Kingdom Foundations* (pages 63–73).

2. Jon Ruthven, "The 'Imitation of Christ' in Christian Tradition: Its Missing Charismatic Emphasis," *Journal of Pentecostal Theology* 16, (2000).

3. Jon Ruthven, *On the Cessation of the Charismata*, 2nd ed. (Tulsa: Word & Spirit Press, 2011), 185–186.

4. Ibid.

5. Ibid.

6. Ibid.

7. For more information about Leif Hetland and his ministry, see www.leif hetlandministries.com and www.globalmissionsawareness.com.

8. Steve Stewart, *When Everything Changes* (Abbotsford, BC: Freshwind Publishing, 2012), 13.

9. Steve Stewart, *Impact Nations* newsletter, May 2006.

10. Steve Stewart, "The 'Ripples' from the Nakuru Prison Baptism Tank Keep Growing," (May 29, 2012), http://network.impactnations.com/profiles/blogs/the-ripples-from-the-nakuru-prison-baptism-tank-keep-growing.

11. For more stories about Steve Stewart and his ministry, see his book *When Everything Changes: Healing, Justice and the Kingdom of God* (Freshwind Publishing, 2012), or visit www.impactnations.com.

12. For more information about the Longs and Catch the Fire USA, see www.catchthefireusa.com.

Chapter 7: Radical Obedience: Impartation for the Power to Die

1. This quote and the ones that follow regarding the cholera outbreak come from the article "Dangerous Cholera Outbreak/God's Response," *Iris Ministries, Inc.* newsletter, February 28, 2001. See www.irismin.org/news/newsletters/view/dangerous-cholera-outbreak-gods-response.

2. Rolland and Heidi Baker, "Congo and Beyond," *Iris Ministries, Inc.* newsletter, June 7, 2005.

Chapter 8: Clothed with Power: Nobody Is Safe!

1. This prophecy was given in much more detail by the prophet Paul Cain. He received it more than 25 times as an open vision. I have also met two other men from different regions of the country and one from another country who have had the exact same vision.

2. For a brief overview of how Pentecostalism spread and the importance of impartation to the early leaders, see *In the Latter Days* by Dr. Vinson Synan (Xulon Press, 2001), and *2000 Years of Charismatic Christianity* by Dr. Eddie Hyatt (Charisma House, 2002). This latter book also shows how Satan's main strategy to fight the anointing is to call it of Satan. I call this the Beelzebub controversy.

3. This movement was called the "Latter Rain," a term which had also been used by the earlier Pentecostals. For a good understanding of this movement, see *Latter Rain: The Latter Rain Movement of 1948 and the Mid-Twentieth Century Evangelical Awakening* by Dr. Richard Riss (Honeycomb Visual Productions, 1987). Some leaders did go into areas of unorthodoxy, but this did not characterize the entire movement. Sadly, however, the Pentecostal denominations of that day rejected the entire movement. In my opinion, they experienced as a result very little of the anointing in prophecy that was a major part of this movement.

4. For more on Pastor Henry Madava and his ministry, visit www.victory church.org.ua.

5. This figure is based on information from our International Ministries department as of February 2011.

6. Global Awakening presently offers four Schools of Healing and Impartation. 1. Revival Phenomena and Healing, (now renamed Foundations) 2. Disbelief,

Deliverance, and Deception, (now renamed Empowerment), 3. Spiritual and Medical Perspectives, 4. Faith and Healing. One more four-day schools will soon be offered: Healing: Christian and New Age. These are four-day schools held in the English-speaking world. For information and location visit our website, www .globalawakening.com.

Chapter 9: The Heritage of the Saints: Impartation and Visitation

1. Justin Martyr, "The Second Apology of Justin for the Christians" (addressed to the Roman Senate: ca. 161 A.D.), www.earlychristianwritings.com/text/ justinmartyr-secondapology.html. Note that for this and other citations in this chapter that come from the Early Christian Writings website and similar sites, the quoted passage can be found by going to the link mentioned and hitting the "Ctrl" and "F" buttons simultaneously on a PC ("Command" and "F" on a Mac). This brings up the find-and-replace search feature. Type a phrase from the passage into the text box and hit "enter." This will enable you to search the entire document quickly and easily to find the desired passage and surrounding material.

2. Hermas, "The Shepherd of Hermas" III.X.4 in *The Apostolic Fathers*, trans. Archbishop William Wake (Edinburgh: John Grant, 1909), 1:299. See also www .earlychristianwritings.com/text/shepherd.html.

3. Morton Kelsey, *Healing and Christianity: A Classic Study* (Minneapolis: Augsburg Fortress, 1995), 118–119. Note that while I am not in agreement with the latter part of Kelsey's book, which analyzes healing from a Jungian psychological framework, I recommend it for its thorough historical documentation of healing ministry accounts in Church history.

4. Tertullian, *To Scapula* (Carthage: ca. 217 AD), www.earlychristianwritings .com/text/tertullian05.html. Tertullian was one of the three greatest theologians of the first twelve hundred years of the Church, along with Augustine and Aquinas. However, later in his life he joined the unorthodox Montanists. The quote is from his orthodox period of ministry.

5. Kelsey, *Healing and Christianity*, 119.

6. Ibid., no page. See also website information at note 7.

7. Origen, "Contra Celsus," (Alexandria: ca. 248 AD), www.earlychristian writings.com/text/origen161.html.

8. Morton Kelsey, *Healing and Christianity: In Ancient Thought and Modern Times* (San Francisco: Harper & Row, 1976), 150. See also Irenaeus, "Against Heresies" (Gaul: ca. 180 AD), www.columbia.edu/cu/augustine/arch/irenaeus.

9. Ibid., 151, and see 148–152.

10. Ibid., 149.

11. Ibid., 185. See also St. Augustine's *Retractationum*.

12. Ibid. See also St. Augustine's *Retractationum*.

13. For more on this, see my School of Healing and Impartation workbook *Deliverance, Disbelief, and Deception* (Mechanicsburg, Penn.: Global Awakening, 2009), 102–103.

14. Kelsey, *Healing and Christianity: In Ancient Thought and Modern Times*, 204–205.

15. Ibid., 219–220.

16. Henry Worsley, *The Life of Martin Luther in Two Volumes* (London: Bell and Daldy, 1856), 2:286–288.

17. Theodore J. Tappert, *Luther: Letters of Spiritual Counsel* (Vancouver, BC: Regent College Publishing, 1960, 2003), 48–49.

18. Thomas Boys, *The Suppressed Evidence: Or Proofs of the Miraculous Faith and Experience of the Church of Christ in All Ages*. This work is available in several reprinted versions.

19. Jonathan Edwards, *The Works of Jonathan Edwards*, vol. 1 (Carlisle, Penn.: Banner of Truth Trust, 1995). See also www.ccel.org/ccel/edwards/works1.txt.

20. Guy Chevreau, *Catch the Fire* (Toronto: HarperCollins, 1995), 177.

21. Ibid., 78–79.

22. Edwards, *The Works*, I.lxviib.

23. Ibid., 86–88.

24. Ibid., 90.

25. This insight comes from Dr. Lewis Drummond, my professor of evangelism at The Southern Baptist Theological Seminary in Louisville from 1975–1977. Also, Dr. Vinson Synan confirmed in a lecture he gave in 1994 in St. Louis (where I held a Catch the Fire conference) that the first Great Awakening was called the "Great Clamor."

26. Chevreau, *Catch the Fire*, 92, quoting from Edwards, *The Works*, I.lxiva.

27. *The Works of John Wesley: Complete and Unabridged*, 3rd ed. (Grand Rapids: Baker, 1991), 1:175.

28. Ibid., 187.

29. Ibid.

30. Ibid., 188.

31. Ibid., 189.

32. Ibid., 190.

33. Ibid., 210.

34. George Whitefield, *George Whitefield's Journals: A new edition containing fuller material than any hitherto published* (Carlisle, Penn.: Banner of Truth Trust, 1960), 263.

35. Clare G. Weakley Jr. ed., *The Nature of Revival: John Wesley, Charles Wesley, & George Whitefield* (Minneapolis: Bethany House, 1987), passim.

36. Nancy A. Hardesty, *Faith Cure: Divine Healing in the Holiness and Pentecostal Movements* (Peabody, Mass.: Hendrickson Publishers, 2003).

37. Lewis Drummond and John Havlik, *How Spiritual Awakenings Happen* (Nashville: The Sunday School Board of the Southern Baptist Convention, 1981), 15.

38. Paul K. Conkin, *Cane Ridge: America's Pentecost* (Madison: University of Wisconsin Press, 1990).

39. For more information, see my School of Healing and Impartation workbook *Revival Phenomena and Healing* (Mechanicsburg, Penn.: Global Awakening, 2008), 7–16.

40. Conkin, *Cane Ridge*, 23.

41. Ibid., 24.

42. Lewis Drummond, *The Awakening That Must Come* (Nashville: Broadman Press, 1978), 16–17.

43. Lewis Drummond and John Havlik, *How Spiritual Awakenings Happen* (Nashville: Sunday School Board of the Southern Baptist Convention, 1981).

44. Peter Cartwright, *Autobiography of Peter Cartwright*, ed. Charles L. Wallis (Nashville: Abingdon, 1956), 12.

45. Ibid., 45.

46. Ibid., 46. See also page 10 of my School of Healing and Impartation workbook *Revival Phenomena*.

47. Charles Finney, *Charles G. Finney: An Autobiography* (Old Tappan, New Jersey: Revell, 1876, 1908), 20–21. See also page 16 of my School of Healing and Impartation workbook *Revival Phenomena*.

48. Finney, *Autobiography*, 21.

49. See page 5 of my workbook *Revival Phenomena*.

50. In 1994, I had my church secretary call all the Southern Baptist seminaries and ask their professors of evangelism this question.

51. Mary Crawford, *The Shantung Revival: The Greatest Revival in Baptist Church History* (Mechanicsburg, Penn.: Global Awakening, 2005).

52. Synan, lecture on revival.

53. I graduated in December 1977 and do not know if this has been rectified since or not.

54. At least, they were not mentioned in my four years of religious studies in college and three years in seminary, including the special class on revival taught by Dr. Drummond.

55. Hardesty, *Faith Cure*, passim.

56. Kelsey, *Healing and Christianity*, 145.

57. Hardesty, *Faith Cure*, passim.

58. Letter from Stephen Olford, May 9, 1996; cf. Marshall Frady, *Billy Graham* (Boston, Little Brown: 1979).

Chapter 10: Winds of Change: Preparation for Restoration

1. Vincent Synan, *In the Latter Days: The Outpouring of the Holy Spirit in the Twentieth Century* (Fairfax, Virg.: Xulon Press, 2001), 31.

2. Ibid., 32.

3. Charles Spurgeon, "The Power of the Holy Spirit" (sermon given June 17, 1855), www.spurgeon.org/sermons/0030.htm.

4. Most present scholarship regarding Kenyon attributes some of the origins of his beliefs to the New Thought heresy of New England. An example of this would be Stanley M. Burgess, Gary B. McGee, and Patrick H. Alexander, *The Dictionary of Pentecostal and Charismatic Movements* (Grand Rapids: Zondervan, 1988), 374. However, this is based upon the faulty research of D. R. McConnell, *A Different Gospel* (Peabody, Mass.: Hendrickson Publishers, 1988). The excellent book *E. W. Kenyon: The Man and His Message of Faith, the True Story* by Joe McIntyre thoroughly disproves this theory based upon faulty conjectures and faulty time lines of Kenyon's life. McIntyre's book is a must read for anyone who wants to understand the true source of the Word of Faith origins. Time does not allow me to prove his point, which McIntyre does so completely, but let me just state that the origins of Kenyon's thought were in great evangelical leaders of the

day. These were men like A. J. Gordon, the Baptist pastor who read the Bible every morning for devotions from the Greek text, A. B. Simpson, a Presbyterian and founder of the Christian & Missionary Alliance, A. T. Pierson, D. L. Moody, R. A. Torrey, Andrew Murray, et. al. In his book *Only Believe*, Dr. Paul King concurs with McIntyre in regard to Kenyon's source of influence being evangelical rather than New Thought. See Joe McIntyre, *E. W. Kenyon: The Man and His Message of Faith, the True Story* (Orlando, FL: Creation House, 1997), passim, and Paul L. King, *Only Believe* (Tulsa: Word & Spirit Press, 2008), 64.

5. David Pytches, *Prophecy in the Local Church* (Great Britian: Hodder and Stougton, 1993), 221.

6. Timothy L. Smith, *Called Unto Holiness: The Story of the Nazarenes: The Formative Years* (Kansas City, Mo: Nazarene Publishing House, 1962), 97. As quoted from E. A. Girvin, P. F. Bresee, *A Prince in Israel* (Kansas City, Mo: Beacon Hill Press, 1916), 82–83.

7. Monsignor Vincent M. Walsh, *What Is Going On? Understanding the Powerful Evangelism of Pentecostal Churches* (Wynnewood, Penn.: Key of David Publications, 1995), 158–162.

8. Ibid.

9. Ibid.

10. Ibid.

11. Andrew Brown, "The Holy Spirit Hits South Kensington," *The Independent*, June 21, 1994.

12. Pope John Paul II, *Veritatis Splendor*, 1993; see www.catholic-pages.com /documents/veritatis_splendor.pdf.

13. Ralph Martin, *The Catholic Church at the End of an Age: What Is the Spirit Saying?* (San Francisco, Calif.: Ignatius Press, 1994), 111.

Chapter 11: Building Bridges so Others Might Receive

1. Thomas Aquinas wanted to reach the Muslims, whose society would come out of the Dark Ages before Christian Europe. They had switched their philosophy of life from neoplatonic to Aristotelian. Aquinas attempted to rewrite Christian theology from the Aristotelian viewpoint in order to reach them. This work became known as his *Summa Theologica* and would become the basis for all Catholic theology for the next several hundred years. It still has a prominent place in Catholic theology today.

2. For a better understanding of the historical development of this dispensationalist doctrine or system of biblical interpretation, see journalist Dave MacPherson's *The Late Great Pre-Trib Rapture* (Heart of America Bible Society, 1974). This relationship has been denied by Darbyites, but this writer believes it has been proven by MacPherson's research. Most historians have not recognized that Edward Irving believed in the pre-trib rapture prior to J. N. Darby; neither do they recognize that Irving was influenced by a Jesuit priest who wrote as a "supposed" converted Jew. This Jesuit was trying to deal with the Protestant commentators of the sixteenth century, the time he lived in, seeing the Pope as the Antichrist and the Catholic Church as the great Whore of Babylon. Irving did not realize the book that influenced him was written by a Roman Catholic. Neither did J. N. Darby.

This information is in the following dispensational articles that were not written by MacPherson, but by an anonymous writer called "a gospel preacher." Here are the best resources I have ever found on dispensationalism:

Dave McPhearson, "Edward Irving Is Unnerving," http://www.scionofzion.com/edward_irving.htm.

A Gospel Preacher, "Dispensationalism—History," http://regal-network.com/dispensationalism/.

A Gospel Preacher, "Dispensationalism—Doctrines," http://regal-network.com/dispensationalism/doctrines.htm.

A Gospel Preacher, "Dispensationalism—Links," http://regal-network.com/dispensationalism/links.htm.

A Gospel Preacher, "Dispensationalism—PDFs," http://regal-network.com/dispensationalism/pdfs.htm.

3. I address the development of cessationism and Warfield's arguments in much greater detail in the lectures I give as part of Global Awakening's Healing School II curriculum: "B. B. Warfield, His Counterfeit Miracles, and Today's Echoes: Introduction to Cessationism," and "B. B. Warfield, His Counterfeit Miracles, and Today's Echoes: Understanding the Historical and Biblical Weaknesses." You can read pages 29–43 and 61–84 of our School of Healing and Impartation workbook: *Deliverance, Disbelief, and Deception* (Global Awakening, 2006) for more information.

4. If you do not want to read the book, you can get a more popular perspective from our *School of Healing and Impartation Workbook II* and/or the accompanying lectures.

5. Jon Ruthven, *On the Cessation of the Charismata: The Protestant Polemic on Postbiblical Miracles* (Sheffield, England: Sheffield Acadmic Press, 1993, 1997, 2011), 77.

Conclusion: Living Out Impartation

1. Graham, *Holy Spirit*, 220.

Bibliography

Baker, H.A. *Visions Beyond the Veil*. Lancaster, UK: Sovereign World, 2006.

Baker, Heidi. *Compelled by Love*. Lake Mary, Fla.: Charisma House, 2008.

Baker, Rolland, interview by Randy Clark. September 2010.

Baker, Rolland, and Heidi Baker, interview by Randy Clark. 1995.

———. *Always Enough*. Grand Rapids: Chosen, 2003.

———. "Dangerous Cholera Outbreak/God's Response." *Iris Ministries, Inc.* newsletter, February 28, 2001. www.irismin.org/news/news letters/view/dangerous-cholera-outbreak-gods-response (accessed 2011 24-September).

———. "Floods, Famine and Harvest in Mozambique." *Iris Ministries, Inc.* newsletter. April 18, 2000.

———. "North to the Zambezi." *Iris Ministries, Inc.* newsletter. May 30, 2000.

———. "Congo and Beyond." *Iris Ministries, Inc.* newsletter. June 7, 2005.

Baker, Rolland, and Supresa Sithole, interview by Randy Clark.

Beverly, James A. *Revival Wars: A Critique of Counterfeit Revival*. Evangelical Research Ministries, 1997.

Boardman, George Dana. *The Kingdom: The Emerging Rule of Christ Among Men: The Original Classic* by George Dana Boardman. Edited by Bob Mumford and Jack Taylor. Shippensburg, Penn.: Destiny Image, 2008.

Brown, Andrew. "The Holy Spirit Hits South Kensington." *The Independent*, June 21, 1994.

Burgess, Stanley M., Gary B. McGee, and Patrick H. Alexander. *The Dictionary of Pentecostal and Charismatic Movements*. Grand Rapids: Zondervan, 1988.

Cartwright, Peter. *Autobiography of Peter Cartwright: The Backwoods Preacher*. Ann Arbor: University of Michigan Library, 2005.

Chevreau, Guy. *Catch the Fire*. Northampton, England: Marshall Pickering, 1994.

Clark, Randy. *Lighting Fires*. Mechanicsburg, Penn: Global Awakening, 2011.

———. *God Can Use Little Ole Me*. Shippensburg, Penn.: Destiny Image Publishers, 1998.

———. School of Healing and Impartation Workbook: *Deliverance, Disbelief, and Deception*. Mechanicsburg, Penn.: Global Awakening, 2006.

———. School of Healing and Impartation Workbook: *Revival Phenomena and Healing*. Mechanicsburg, Penn: Global Awakening, 2008.

———. School of Healing and Impartation Workbook: *Spiritual and Medical Perspectives*. Mechanicsburg, Penn.: Global Awakening, 2008.

———. *Changed in a Moment*. Mechanicsburg, Penn.: Global Awakening, 2010.

———. *Power, Holiness, and Evangelism: Rediscovering God Purity, Power, and Passion for the Lost*. Shippensburg, Penn.: Destiny Image, 1999.

Conkin, Paul K. *Cane Ridge: America's Pentecost*. Madison: University of Wisconsin Press, 1990.

Cooke, Graham, interview by Randy Clark. Prior to 2000.

Crawford, Mary. *The Shantung Revival*. Mechanicsburg, Penn.: Global Awakening, 2005.

Culpepper, Robert. *An Evaluation of the Charismatic Movement: A Theological and Biblical Appraisal*. Valley Forge, Penn.: Judson Press, 1977.

DeArteaga, William. *Quenching the Spirit: Examining Centuries of Opposition to the Moving of the Holy Spirit*. Lake Mary, Fla.: Creation House, 1992.

Drummond, Lewis A. *The Awakening That Must Come*. Nashville: Broadman Press, 1978.

Dunn, James D. G. *Jesus and the Spirit: A Study of the Religious and Charismatic Experience of Jesus and the First Christians as Reflected in the New Testament*. Grand Rapids: Eerdmans, 1997.

Edwards, Jonathan. *The Works of Jonathan Edwards*, vol. 1. www.ccel.org/ccel/edwards/works1.txt.

Fee, Gordon D. *God's Empowering Presence: The Holy Spirit in the Letters of Paul.* Grand Rapids: Baker Academic, 2009.

———. *Paul, the Spirit, and the People of God.* Peabody, Mass: Hendrickson Publishers, 1996.

Finney, Charles G. *Charles G. Finney: An Autobiography.* Old Tappan, N.J: Revell, 1876, 1908.

———. *Revivals of Religion,* A 700 Club Edition. Originally published as *Lectures on Revivals of Religion.* Virginia Beach, Va.: CBN University Press, 1978.

Galli, Pastor Silvio, interview by Randy Clark. 2003.

Graham, Billy. *The Holy Spirit: Activating God's Power in Your Life.* Waco: Word Books, 1978.

Girvin, E. A. *P. F. Bresee, a Prince in Israel.* Kansas City, Miss.: Beacon Hill Press, 1916.

Hanegraaff, Wouter J. *New Age Religion and Western Culture: Esotericism in the Mirror of Secular Thought.* Albany, NY: State University of New York Press, 1998.

Hardesty, Nancy A. *Faith Cure: Divine Healing in the Holiness and Pentecostal Movements.* Peabody, Mass.: Hendrickson Publishers, Inc., 2003.

Hattaway, Paul. *Back to Jerusalem: Three Chinese House Church Leaders Share Their Vision to Complete the Great Commission.* Portland, Ore.: Gabriel Publishing, 2003.

Havlik, John, and Lewis A. Drummond. "How Spiritual Awakenings Happen." Nashville: The Sunday School Board of the Southern Baptist Convention, 1981.

Helfin, Ruth. "Prophetic Word Given to Randy Clark at Deliverance Evangelistic Church." Philadelphia, Penn: 1996.

Hermas. *The Shepherd of Hermas.* www.earlychristianwritings.com/text/shepherd.html.

Hilborn, David, ed. *"Toronto" in Perspective: Papers on the New Charismatic Wave of the Mid 1990's.* London, UK: Acute, 2001.

Hume, David. *On Miracles.* Chicago: Open Court Publishing Company, 1986.

Hyatt, Eddie L. *2000 Years of Charismatic Christianity.* Dallas: Hyatt International Ministries, Inc., 1998.

Iranaeus. *Against Heresies.* www.columbia.edu/cu/augustine/arch/irenaeus.

Johnson, Bill. *When Heaven Invades Earth: A Practical Guide to a Life of Miracles.* Shippensburg, Penn.: Destiny Image, 2005.

Kelsey, Morton T. *Healing and Christianity: In Ancient Thought and Modern Times.* San Francisco: Harper & Row, 1976.

Kimn, Dayoung, interview by Randy Clark.

King, Paul L. *Only Believe: Examining the Origin and Development of Classic and Contemporary Word of Faith Theologies.* Tulsa: Word & Spirit Press, 2008.

Ladd, George Eldon. *Gospel and the Kingdom: Scriptural Studies in the Kingdom of God.* Grand Rapids: Eerdmans, 1990.

Lindsell, Harold. *The Holy Spirit in the Latter Days.* Nashville: Thomas Nelson, 1983.

Long, Stacy. Email to Randy Clark. 2011.

MacPherson, Dave. *The Late Great Pre-Trib Rapture.* Kansas City, Miss.: Heart of America Bible Society, 1974.

Martin, Ralph. *The Catholic Church at the End of an Age: What Is the Spirit Saying?* San Francisco: Ignatius Press, 1994.

Martyr, Justin. *The Second Apology of Justin for the Christians.* www.earlychristianwritings.com/text/justinmartyr-secondapology.html.

McConnell, D. R. *A Different Gospel.* Peabody, Mass.: Hendrickson Publishers, 1988.

McGavarn, Dr. Donald. *Understanding Church Growth.* Grand Rapids: Eerdmans, 1990.

McIntyre, Joe. *E .W. Kenyon: The Man and His Message of Faith, The True Story.* Orlando: Creation House, 1997.

Miller, R. Edward. *Cry for Me Argentina.* Brentwood, Essex: Sharon Publications Ltd, 1988.

Origen. *Contra Celsus.* www.earlychristianwritings.com/text/origen161.html.

Ostling, Richard N., Helen Gibson, and Gavin Scott. "www.Time.com." *TIME magazine* U.S. August 15, 1994. http://www.time.com/time/magazine/article/0,9171,981256,00.html.

Paul, Pope John II. *Veritatis Splendor.* www.catholic-pages.com/documents/veritatis_splendor.pdf.

Peck, George. *Throne Life.* Boston: Watchword, 1888.

Percival, Henry R., ed. *A Select Library of Nicene and Post-Nicene Fathers of the Christian Church.* 2nd series, vol. 14. Grand Rapids: Eerdmans, 1979.

Prankard, Bill, interview with Randy Clark, Catch the Fire TV, Toronto Airport Christian Fellowship. 1994.

Pullinger, Jackie. *Chasing the Dragon.* London, UK: Hodder Religious, 2010.

Pytches, David. *Prophecy in the Local Church.* London, UK: Hodder and Stoughton, 1993.

Riss, Richard. *Latter Rain: The Latter Rain Movement of 1948 and the Mid-Twentieth Century Evangelical Awakening.* Etobicoke, Ontario: Honeycomb Visual Productions Ltd., 1987.

Roberts, Alexander, and James Donaldson. *The Apostolic Fathers with Justin Martyr and Irenaeus*. vol. 1. Grand Rapids: Eerdmans, 1981.

Ruthven, Dr. Jon. "The 'Imitation of Christ' in Christian Tradition: Its Missing Charismatic Emphasis." *Journal of Pentecostal Theology* 16, (2000).

————. *On the Cessation of the Charismata: The Protestant Polemic on Postbiblical Miracles*. Sheffield: Sheffield Academic Press, 1997.

————. *On the Cessation of the Charismata: The Protestant Polemic on Post-biblical Miracles*—Revised and Expanded edition. Tulsa: Word & Spirit Press, 2011.

————. *What's Wrong with Protestant Theology?* Tulsa: Word & Spirit Press, 2011.

Sheridan, Lucas. Letter to Randy Clark entitled "Experience in Annapolis, Brazil." September 6, 2005.

————, interview by Randy Clark. October 2010.

Smith, Timothy L. *Called Unto Holiness: The Story of the Nazarenes: The Formative Years*. Kansas City, Miss.: Nazarene Publishing House, 1962.

Smithers, David. "Count Zinzendorf." *Awake and Go!* Global Prayer Network, 2006. http://www.watchword.org/index.php?option=com_content&task=view&id=48&Itemid=48.

Spurgeon, Charles. *The Power of the Holy Spirit*. www.biblebb.com/files/spurgeon/0030.htm.

Suenens, Leon Joseph. *A New Pentecost*. San Francisco: Harper, 1984.

Synan, Dr. Vinson. "Lecture on Revival." St. Louis, Miss.: Catch the Fire Conference, 1994.

————. *In the Latter Days: The Outpouring of the Holy Spirit in the Twentieth Century*. Fairfax, Va: Xulan Press, 2001.

Tappert, Theodore, J. *Luther: Letters of Spiritual Counsel*. Vancouver, BC: Regent College Publishing, 1960, 2003.

Tertullian. *To Scapula*. www.earlychristianwritings.com/text/tertullian05.html.

Walsh, Vincent M. *Experiencing Revival in the Catholic Church: What God Is Doing in Our Midst—A Story of God's Initiative and Special Actions*. Wynnewood, Penn.: Key of David Publications, 1995.

————. *What Is Going On? Understanding the Powerful Evangelism of Pentecostal Churches*. Wynnewood, Penn.: Key of David Publications, 1995.

Weakley, Clare George Jr. ed. *The Nature of Revival*. Minneapolis: Bethany, 1987.

White, Todd, phone interview for Randy Clark. December 2011.

Whitefield, George. *George Whitefield's Journals: A New Edition Containing Fuller Material than Any Hitherto Published.* Carlisle, Penn.: Banner of Truth Trust, 1960.

Wood, Laurence W. *The Meaning of Pentecost in Early Methodism.* Lanham: Scarecrow Press, 2002.

Worsley, Henry. *The Life of Martin Luther in Two Volumes.* London, UK: Bell and Daldy, 1856.

Index

243

tongues. *See* speaking/praying, in tongues
Toronto Airport Christian Fellowship, 127
Toronto Blessing, 37–39, 112, 187
    transferable nature of, 206
Torrey, R. A., 190, 196

Ukraine, 83, 142, 225
Ung, Sophal, 126–127, 128
United States, Protestant hunger for the Holy Spirit and holiness in, 196–199
unity, and diversity, 44–45

"Veni Creator Spiritas" ("Come, Holy Spirit" [Pope Leo XIII]), 201
Veritatis Splendor ("The Splendor of Truth" [Pope John Paul II]), 207–208
Victoria Christian Church, 142

Walsh, Vincent M., 200, 201–203
Warfield, B. B., 214–215
Welsh Revival, 143, 205
Wesley, John, 46, 51, 177–179, 180–181, 221
Western Europe, revival of Christianity in, 141–142
Whitefield, George, 179–181, 181–182, 221
Wigglesworth, Smith, 190, 205, 222
Wilkerson, David, 30
Wimber, John, 29–30, 31–32, 33, 37, 75, 171, 190
Woodward-Etter, Maria, 222
World of Faith Movement, 51
Wright, Sharon, 65

Xavier, Francis, 221

Youth Power Invasion, 144

Zacharias, 88

Randy Clark is best known for helping spark the move of God now affectionately labeled the "Toronto Blessing." In the years since, his influence has grown as an international speaker. He continues, with great tenacity, to demonstrate the Lord's power to heal the sick.

Randy received his M.Div. from the Southern Baptist Theological Seminary and his D.Min. from Phoenix University of Theology. He is presently working on his D.Min. from United Theological Seminary, Dayton, Ohio. His message is simple: "God wants to use you."

The most important aspect of Randy's calling to ministry is the way God uses him for impartation. John Wimber heard God speak audibly the first two times he met Randy, telling John that Randy would one day go around the world laying his hands on pastors and leaders for the impartation and activation of the gifts of the Holy Spirit. In January 1994—the early days of the Spirit's outpouring in Toronto—John called Randy and told him that what God had shown him about Randy ten years earlier was beginning now. It has continued ever since.

Randy has the unique ability to minister to many denominations and apostolic networks. These have included Roman Catholics, Messianic Jews, Methodists, many Pentecostal and charismatic congregations and the largest Baptist churches in Argentina, Brazil and South Africa. He has also taken several thousand people with him on international ministry team trips around the world. Randy has traveled to over 43 countries and continues to travel extensively to see that God's mandate on his life is fulfilled.

Randy is also the founder of the Global School of Supernatural Ministry (GSSM), a training school that equips believers for ministry in a variety of arenas. Randy also started an online certification program offering training in physical healing, inner healing and deliverance. Called the Christian Healing Certification Program (CHCP), it is certified by the Apostolic Network of Global Awakening and by the Institute of Applied Theology of United Theological Seminary in Dayton, Ohio (a United Methodist seminary). Along with GSSM, four on-the-road schools are offered (each four days long) in different locales. Randy is also involved with the Wagner Leadership Institute.

About training for ministry, Randy says, "Do not tell yourself that you cannot be used by God on the mission field or in a ministry of mercy. Many people are shocked at how God is using them in major ways. Just be open to the supernatural power of God that will enable you to live a transformed life of ministry. Consider joining us in the streets of our nation and in the nations of the world and becoming part of the great new missionary expansion in the United States and around the world." Through national events and international mission trips, Global Awakening continually offers many opportunities for people to build up their faith, receive an impartation of the Holy Spirit and minister to others at home and abroad. If you experience a powerful touch from God after reading this book, praying with Randy at the end and waiting upon the Lord, he would like you to contact his office by emailing your testimony to goglobal@globalawakening.com. He would love to hear about your experience and its fruit.

Randy and his wife, DeAnne, reside in Mechanicsburg, Pennsylvania. They have four adult children (three of whom are married) and two grandchildren. For more information about his ministry and his resource materials, visit www.globalawakening.com. For more information about GSSM and CHCP, visit gssm.globalawakening.com and www.healingcertification.com.

Other Books by Randy Clark

Changed in a Moment
Entertaining Angels
The Essential Guide to Healing (co-authored with Bill Johnson)
God Can Use Little Ole Me
Healing Unplugged (co-authored with Bill Johnson)
Lighting Fires
Power, Holiness and Evangelism
Supernatural Missions

Booklets

Acts of Obedience: Relationship to Healing and Miracles
Awed by His Grace/Out of the Bunkhouse
Baptism in the Holy Spirit
Biblical Basis for Healing
Christ in You the Hope of Glory and Healing/ Healing and the Glory
Deliverance

Evangelism Unleashed
Falling Under the Power
Healing Is in the Atonement/The Power of the Lord's Supper
Healing Out of Intimacy with God
The Healing Streams That Make Up the Healing River
Learning to Minister under the Anointing/Healing Ministry in Your Church
Open Heaven
Pressing In/Spend and Be Spent
Thrill of Victory/Agony of Defeat
Words of Knowledge

School of Healing and Impartation Ministry Materials

Ministry Team Training Manual
Deliverance, Deception, Disbelief and Healing
Medical and Spiritual Perspectives
Revival Phenomena and Healing

More Insight From Veteran Healing Leaders Bill Johnson and Randy Clark

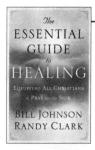

God's miraculous healing is part of the Good News, and you, too, can become a powerful conduit for the healing power He loves to manifest. In this practical, step-by-step guide, Bill Johnson and Randy Clark team up to equip *all* Christians to minister healing.

The Essential Guide to Healing

Listen in as, for the first time, Bill Johnson and Randy Clark sit down to interview each other, candidly sharing their personal journeys behind life in the healing spotlight. With honesty, humor and humility they reveal

- how and why they first got into healing ministry
- the trials, errors and breakthrough experiences that propelled them forward
- the most amazing miracles they've seen
- detailed insights and time-tested advice for more effective ministry

No stages. No spotlights. Just raw, rare, intimate glimpses into real lives—through both the failures and the successes—of two men devoted to God.

Healing Unplugged

Chosen

chosenbooks.com